Especially for

....

From

....

Date

....

180 DEVOTIONS

TO HUSH YOUR

INNER CRITIC

Donna K. Maltese

180 DEVOTIONS

TO HUSH YOUR

INNER CRITIC

Positive Inspiration for Your Heart & Soul

BARBOUR
PUBLISHING

INTRODUCTION

"Can a mother forget the infant at her breast,
walk away from the baby she bore?
But even if mothers forget,
I'd never forget you—never.
Look, I've written your names on the backs of my hands."
ISAIAH 49:15-16 MSG

God adores you like no other. You're so precious to Him that He's tattooed your name on the backs of His hands! He continually exclaims over you, "O my love, how beautiful you are! There is no flaw in you!" (Song of Solomon 4:7 AMPC). He's even written you a love letter—the Bible—sent directly from His heart to yours.

180 Devotions to Hush Your Inner Critic has been written to remind you how much God loves and values you. It contains 180 "glass half-full" devotions, Bible verses, and prayers, all of which end with takeaway faith-boosting statements you can carry with you throughout the day.

To reinforce the truth that you matter to God, each reading's title completes the sentence "You're worthy because. . ." By making this book part of your daily spiritual "diet," you'll remove from your mind any doubts as to how much God loves you. Your heart will be refreshed as you begin to understand the many gifts He lavishes upon you. And the fact that God has plans to prosper you and give you peace (see Jeremiah 29:11) will be salve for your soul.

Enter into these pages today, and let the positive self-talk begin!

GOD CALLS YOU AS HE SEES YOU

And the Angel of the Lord appeared to him and said to him,
The Lord is with you, you mighty man of [fearless] courage.
JUDGES 6:12 AMPC

Sometimes the Lord sees you in a way you do not yet see yourself. That's what happened with Gideon. God saw Gideon as a mighty warrior, a person with fearless courage. Yet Gideon saw himself only as the poorest of his clan and the least in his father's house. But God knew what Gideon would do. He would be a fearless champion because God was with him. He told Gideon, "Surely I will be with you, and you shall smite the Midianites as one man" (Judges 6:16 AMPC). And he did!

Never underestimate who you are. Never doubt how God sees you. Don't let your circumstances dictate your reality. "Go with the strength you have" (Judges 6:14 NLT), never doubting God's power within you.

When God calls you strong, don't think of yourself as weak. When God says you're found, don't see yourself as lost. When God sees you as worthy, don't think of yourself as worthless. Your strength lies in the God who sees you as you truly are: a mighty woman of courage, a beloved daughter through whom He conquers the world (see 1 John 5:4–5).

Help me to see myself as You see me, Lord. I can do anything with You!

I know I'm worthy because God sees who I truly am.

GOD FIGHTS FOR YOU

*"Do not fear or be dismayed because of this great
multitude, for the battle is not yours but God's."*
2 CHRONICLES 20:15 NASB

Enemy armies were lining up to attack King Jehoshaphat. Terrified, he begged God for guidance. He and his people prayed and fasted. Jehoshaphat admitted he couldn't handle the situation, telling God, "We are powerless before this great multitude who are coming against us; nor do we know what to do, but our eyes are on You" (2 Chronicles 20:12 NASB).

Then God spoke through the priest Jahaziel, telling Jehoshaphat not to be afraid or discouraged because the battle wasn't his but God's. God said, "Station yourselves, stand and see the salvation of the LORD on your behalf" (2 Chronicles 20:17 NASB).

With this knowledge in hand and heart, Jehoshaphat led his people out *before his own army*, singing and praising the Lord! The story ends with the enemy armies attacking each other, leaving Jehoshaphat to simply pick up the spoils.

When multitudes are coming against you, there's no need to be fearful or discouraged. Simply keep your eyes on God, knowing He's got you. *He's* fighting your battles. Your job? To praise and follow Him.

---

*Sometimes, Lord, I think my problems are greater than You!
Help me keep my eyes on You alone, to know You have
me covered. And all I have to do is praise!*

I know I'm worthy because my mighty God is fighting my battles.

GOD LOOKS OUT FOR YOU

The Angel of the Lord found her by a spring of water in the wilderness.
GENESIS 16:7 AMPC

In the Old Testament, we find an aging Sarah, who's frustrated that the baby God had promised to her and Abraham hasn't yet materialized. So she comes up with her own plan. Abraham will sleep with her maid, Hagar. Then Sarah will take the resulting child as her own. So Abraham lies with Hagar, who gets pregnant and soon assumes a sense of superiority over Sarah.

Sarah, now despising Hagar, sends her away. The maid runs into the wilderness and sits down by a well. That's where the angel of the Lord finds her. He asks her what's happening. After Hagar gives her version of events, the angel tells her to go back to her mistress, that God will bless Hagar. That "the Lord has heard and paid attention" (Genesis 16:11 AMPC) to her problem.

In response, Hagar says, "You are the God who sees me" (Genesis 16:13 NLT). "That's how that desert spring got named 'God-Alive-Sees-Me Spring'" (Genesis 16:14 MSG).

The point? Know you're never alone. No matter where you go, God is concerned about what's happening in your life. Your God who sees is always looking out for you, ready to help, to guide, and to bless.

---

*Thank You for always being with me, Lord,
even during wilderness moments.*

I know I'm worthy because my God is looking out for me.

GOD EASES YOUR JOURNEY

*He caused the storm to be still, so that the waves of the
sea were hushed. Then they were glad because they
were quiet, so He guided them to their desired haven.*
PSALM 107:29–30 NASB

The Old Testament verses above were brought to life in the New (see John 6:15–21). Jesus had just fed more than five thousand people with five loaves of bread and two fish. Then He withdrew to a hillside to pray alone.

Meanwhile, His disciples went down to the sea to row over to Capernaum. Darkness had descended, and the winds began to blow, making the sea rough, the waves high. Then the God-followers saw Jesus walking on the sea toward them and became terrified.

> *But Jesus said to them, It is I; be not afraid! [I AM; stop
> being frightened!] Then they were quite willing and glad
> for Him to come into the boat. And now the boat went at
> once to the land they had steered toward. [And immedi-
> ately they reached the shore toward which they had been
> slowly making their way.]* John 6:20–21 AMPC

When you're faced with wind and waves, don't fear. Simply be willing, glad to invite Jesus into your boat. Before you know it, He'll bring you to the place you were struggling to reach.

---

*With You in my boat, Jesus, I no longer struggle,
for You whisk me to my desired haven.*

I know I'm worthy because my God eases my journey.

GOD'S SPIRIT STANDS WITH YOU

*Be strong, alert, and courageous, all you people of the land, says the
Lord, and work! For I am with you, says the Lord of hosts. . . .
My Spirit stands and abides in the midst of you; fear not.*
HAGGAI 2:4-5 AMPC

● ● ● ● ● ● ● ● ● ● ● ● ● ● ●

More than five hundred years before Christ was born, King Cyrus of Persia
allowed the exiled Jews to return to Israel to rebuild the temple that had been
destroyed. Two years later they began the work, but because of opposition
from neighbors and the indifference by the Jews, they abandoned the effort.
After sixteen years had passed, God spoke through the prophet Haggai,
telling His people to be strong and not fear, to finish the work because He
was with them and His Spirit was standing in their midst. Because of God's
encouragement, His people completed the temple four years later.

When you're plagued with discouragement and others oppose your efforts,
remember that God wants you to take His courage and strength and do the
work He's given you to do. Be alert to the fact that God has given you His
Holy Spirit to stand *with* you and live *in* you.

---

*Lord, when my spirit lags, keep me alert to the fact that Your
Spirit is with and in me. Give me the courage and the oomph
to do just what You want me to do, in Jesus' name. Amen.*

I know I'm worthy because God and His Spirit stand with me.

GOD MEETS YOUR NEEDS

"What I'm trying to do here is to get you to relax, to not be so preoccupied with getting, so you can respond to God's giving. . . . Steep your life in God-reality, God-initiative, God-provisions. Don't worry about missing out. You'll find all your everyday human concerns will be met."

MATTHEW 6:32–33 MSG

Jesus knows just how easy it is for us to forget about God's love and care for us. We, at times, may find ourselves so busy working to make ends meet that we forget to seek His face. That's why He gave us these invaluable words.

Relax. Look at what God is doing around you. Before you step into your home office, start cleaning the house, begin that long commute, or wake up the kids—stop. Spend some time with God. Open up His Book, ingest His words of wisdom, pray with all your heart, and open yourself to His presence. Steep yourself in *His* reality. See all that happens through *His* eyes.

Seek God's kingdom above and before all else, and you will not only find Him meeting all your needs but you'll find your cup running over with blessings you never dreamed imaginable.

I'm here, Lord, steeping myself in Your reality, knowing You love me so much I will always have all I need!

I know I'm worthy because God always meets my needs.

GOD BUSIES HIMSELF WITH YOUR EVERY STEP

The steps of a [good] man are directed and established by the
Lord when He delights in his way [and He busies Himself with
his every step]. Though he falls, he shall not be utterly cast down,
for the Lord grasps his hand in support and upholds him.
PSALM 37:23–24 AMPC

• • • • • • • • • • • • • • • • •

When you live a godly life—obeying God and His Word—God will not only direct your steps but will pave the way for you, busying Himself with every step you make! And when you're in that place, you can hear His voice behind you at every crossroad, saying, "This is the way; walk in it" (Isaiah 30:21 AMPC).

When you're that close to God, He's close to you—so close that even if you fall while on that God-directed path, whether it's because you hit an unexpected pothole or because you tripped up by momentarily veering away, He'll be there to grab you, pull you up, and get you back on your feet!

So never fear when you're walking in God's ways. Just stick your foot out in faith, knowing God is busying Himself with your every step.

Lord, I want You to be delighted with where I'm going. Help me
begin by following Your will, way, and Word, knowing You'll be blazing
the trail before me. All I have to do is follow Your love and light.

I know I'm worthy because my God
busies Himself with every step I take.

15

GOD GIVES YOU SAFETY, SECURITY, AND GUIDANCE

I waited patiently for the LORD; and He inclined to me and heard my cry. He brought me up out of the pit of destruction, out of the miry clay, and He set my feet upon a rock making my footsteps firm.

PSALM 40:1-2 NASB

Some days you may find yourself in a pit of despair. When you're in that dark place, wait patiently for God to draw you back out into His light. Expect Him to show up to save you. Cry out, knowing He *will* hear your voice and be there before you even utter your first word.

And when God gets there—and He *will* get there—He'll not only save you by pulling you out of the pit, He'll secure you by setting your feet on firm ground. Then He'll guide your next steps, ensuring they'll be steady and solid. Safety, security, and guidance from the Creator of the universe, the one who gives you breath, who keeps your world in orbit. What more could a woman need or want?

Wait patiently for God to come when you call, precious one. He'll be there before you can say, "Thank God!"

I'm overcome with peace, Lord, knowing You hear my cry before it even reaches my lips. Thank You for being my Savior, my security, and my guide!

I know I'm worthy because my God pulls me up, sets me on solid ground, and steadies my steps.

GOD OPENS DOORS

"Keep on asking, and you will receive what you ask for. Keep on seeking, and you will find. Keep on knocking, and the door will be opened to you. For everyone who asks, receives. Everyone who seeks, finds. And to everyone who knocks, the door will be opened."
MATTHEW 7:7–8 NLT

Jesus tells you that just as a good parent gives her child what he asks for, knowing it will be good for her little one, "the God who conceived you in love" (Matthew 7:11 MSG) will be sure to give you what *you* desire. The thing is to keep on asking, and then keep on seeking that which you've asked for. At the same time, keep on knocking on God's door, expecting Him to open it to you!

The God who loves you *wants* you to actively come to Him. Never hesitate to ask Him for the things you need. Do not give up. The more you ask Him, the more you're cutting to the core of what you truly desire.

So keep asking, seeking, and knocking. Father God is waiting to bless you.

Loving God, You're the one I can always count on to deliver what I need. Help me hone my desires, lining them up with Your will and way. Give me the patience and persistence I need to keep on coming to the one I can count on.

I know I'm worthy because my loving
God opens the door to my desires.

GOD GIVES YOU JUSTICE

Many crave and seek the ruler's favor, but the
wise man [waits] for justice from the Lord.
PROVERBS 29:26 AMPC

When things don't go their way, children usually pout and say aloud, "That's not fair!" And lots of times they're right. Know the feeling?

When things don't go your way, when someone or some institution blindsides you or unexpectedly pulls the rug out from under your feet, you may be thinking, *That's not fair!* And you may be right. But rather than seeking revenge or craving to get some bigwig's attention so you can plead your case, why not take the wiser course? Calm down, and wait for God to make things right. After all, that's what He wants you to do. Instead of holding a grudge, bless those who have harmed you. Leave in God's hands that which He wants you to leave there. Let Him be your guide. He loves you too much to ever steer you wrong.

Be a wise woman. Wait for God to make things right.

Lord, sometimes I find it difficult to wait for You to act. Give me
the patience to do so, knowing You're watching over me. You want
the best for me. And You'll make everything work out just as You
planned so I don't have to worry. I only need to wait. . .for You.

I know I'm worthy because I'm a wise woman who
trusts God will make all things right.

GOD GIVES YOU A SPIRIT OF POWER

For God did not give us a spirit of timidity (of cowardice, of craven and cringing and fawning fear), but [He has given us a spirit] of power and of love and of calm and well-balanced mind and discipline and self-control.

2 TIMOTHY 1:7 AMPC

●　●　●　●　●　●　●　●　●　●　●　●　●　●　●　●

No matter what comes against you, you need fear nothing. Your loving God has gifted you the spirit of power, giving you the courage to face anything and everything in your life. And His provision doesn't end there. He also gifts you the spirit of love for Him, yourself, and others so you'll have the eagerness to serve without fear. He gifts you with the spirit of calm so you won't be steered wrong by your imagination, which may lead you off course.

Yes, woman, dearly loved, God has given you all the spiritual resources you need to not just survive but thrive in this world—and beyond—for Him.

Today, spend some time meditating on your spirit of power, love, and calm. Realize you have everything you need to do what God has called you to do . . .and nothing at all to fear.

I come to You, Lord, leaning into You, tapping into the spirit of power, love, and calmness You have gifted me so I can answer Your call, whatever it may be, wherever it may lead.

I know I'm worthy because God has gifted me with a spirit of power, love, and calm.

GOD'S PLAN FOR YOU

"I know what I'm doing. I have it all planned out—plans to take care of you, not abandon you, plans to give you the future you hope for."
JEREMIAH 29:11 MSG

Whether you're conscious of it or not, you're always making plans. From the time you get out of bed in the morning to the time you lie down at night, you're making mental notes about what your next step, task, duty, or goal will be. Yet, at times, you may not be sure of your next step. Or you may find your plans have gone awry and you need to make a new plan.

No matter what's happening in your life, you need not feel as if God has left you to navigate this journey alone. Know that He has a master plan for you. And even if it looks as if things aren't going your way, relax. They're going *God's* way, according to His plan—which includes taking care of you and always being with you, working to give you the future you're hoping for.

So, although it's still good to make your plans, remember God will have His way. And every way He chooses for you is the right one.

Thank You, God, for making me a part of Your master plan. I can relax knowing it's You who is in control. Show me what—if anything—You would have me do next.

I know I'm worthy because God has included me in His wonderful plan.

GOD SHOWS YOU HIS GOODNESS

*I would have despaired unless I had believed that I would
see the goodness of the LORD in the land of the living.
Wait for the LORD; be strong and let your heart take courage.*
PSALM 27:13–14 NASB

When life gets rough, when you're in crisis mode, when you see no way out of the dark place you find yourself in, you can always hang on to one thing: you have a God who will show you His goodness in some way in this life. He has things waiting for you, blessings that are (or perhaps have already appeared) just around the corner.

For now, while you're in the midst of your trouble, let God hide you "in His shelter; in the secret place of His tent. . .high upon a rock" (Psalm 27:5 AMPC). Know that even if those closest to you desert you, God will hold you close (see Psalm 27:10). And He'll lead you on a level path when you're ready (see Psalm 27:11). All you need to do is wait on God. To be strong and have courage while doing so. There's nothing He won't do for you, no goodness He'll not reveal in His time.

---

*I'm believing that I'll see Your goodness in my life, Lord.
So I'm taking heart while I wait in Your strength and love.*

I know I'm worthy because God has something good waiting for me.

21

GOD GUARDS AND KEEPS YOU IN PERFECT PEACE

You will guard him and keep him in perfect and constant peace whose mind [both its inclination and its character] is stayed on You, because he commits himself to You, leans on You, and hopes confidently in You.
ISAIAH 26:3 AMPC

Your relationship with God is a two-way street. When you believe you matter to Him, when you give Him your trust, He will guard you, allowing nothing to touch or unsettle you. When you keep your mind and focus on Him, living for, leaning on, and loving Him, He will keep you in perpetual peace. That's a peace that reigns within and outside of you.

Know that God is not some distant spiritual entity that only checks on you once in a while. You're constantly on His mind. He's continually looking out for you, looking to see what you need, how He can help. As you lean into that knowledge and keep your eyes on Him, confident He will always be there, you cannot help but have that perfect calm. That's why, when bad news hits, you have no fear, for you are confidently trusting in the one who loves you like no other (see Psalm 112:7). Live in that peace. Love it. Cherish it. It's yours for the taking!

I'm setting my sights on You, Lord, trusting You for all. Thank You for the perfect peace that gives me!

I know I'm worthy because God keeps me in perfect peace.

GOD SHEPHERDS YOU

The Lord is my Shepherd [to feed, guide,
and shield me], I shall not lack.
PSALM 23:1 AMPC

God's Word tells you that "We are the people he watches over, the flock under his care" (Psalm 95:7 NLT). So you can be sure God is forever watching you, providing you with all you need. With Him filling your life, there is nothing you lack.

There are no greater words than those of Psalm 23, which detail all God does for you. He feeds, guides, and protects you. He makes you lie down in lush pastures, leading you beside the still waters so you can eat and drink and be refreshed in His presence. He restores you to yourself, leading you down the right paths—and all because He loves you just as you are!

Even during those hard knocks in life, when you feel as if you are walking in shadows, you need not fear, for the Great Shepherd is with you, protecting you with His rod and guiding you with His staff. He even prepares a banquet for you, anointing you with the oil of His Holy Spirit.

Meditate and refresh your spirit with Psalm 23 today. Know, precious lamb, that God's goodness, mercy, and love pursue you every day!

Thank You, Great Shepherd, for the tender care
You give me, Your daughter, Your lamb.

I know I'm worthy because I'm in the care of God, my Great Shepherd.

GOD HELPS AND SHIELDS YOU

Our inner selves wait [earnestly] for the Lord; He is our Help and our Shield. For in Him does our heart rejoice, because we have trusted (relied on and been confident) in His holy name. Let Your mercy and loving-kindness, O Lord, be upon us, in proportion to our waiting and hoping for You.
PSALM 33:20–22 AMPC

The more you wait on and hope in God, the more you trust Him, the more joy you will find as you walk the road He has laid out before you.

Allow yourself to focus on the fact that God's mercy, love, and kindness are constantly upon you. Know that no matter how dark things may appear to be, your Creator is going to make something good come out of it. He's already helping you to stand your ground. He's shielding you from all evils—seen and unseen.

Your job is to trust that God will not just bring you through the stresses, trials, and temptations of your day, He will bring you success *in spite of* them! Why? Because He's your help and your shield. The more you trust in Him, the more you'll not just get *through* life but find true life!

Grow my trust in You, Lord, so that as my inner self learns to wait and hope in You, I find myself pleasantly overwhelmed by the expanse of Your love for me.

I know I'm worthy because Almighty God helps and shields me.

GOD IS YOUR ARM OF STRENGTH AND PROTECTION

O Lord, be gracious to us; we have waited [expectantly] for You. Be the arm [of Your servants—their strength and defense] every morning, our salvation in the time of trouble.

ISAIAH 33:2 AMPC

The Hebrew word for *wait* in the above verse means to depend on and order your activities around a future event—in this instance, God's ultimately fulfilling His promises to you. In the next sentence, *Strong's Concordance* says the Hebrew word for *arm* implies an arm stretched out, which equates to "force—arm, help, might, power, shoulder, strength."

Imagine living your life expecting this promise from God to become your reality. To awaken each morning, praying, "You, oh mighty God, will be my arm, my strength and defense," will not only give you the right mindset as you enter your day but will be a powerful tool throughout it. You can increase the power of this prayer by adding motions to it. Move your arms into a weight-lifting position when saying the word *strength*, and then swing them in front of your face in a boxing defensive position when you say "defense." Then go into your day with confidence, knowing God is with you and the fulfillment of His promise awaits you!

Oh mighty God, be my arm, my strength, and my defense every morning.

I know I'm worthy because Almighty God arms me with power.

GOD VALUES YOU

"What is the price of five sparrows—two copper coins?
Yet God does not forget a single one of them. And the very
hairs on your head are all numbered. So don't be afraid;
you are more valuable to God than a whole flock of sparrows."

LUKE 12:6-7 NLT

One of the first things mothers do is count their newborn's fingers and toes. The mom is intent, focused, and concerned with every detail of her precious child, checking to see where her love, care, and wisdom might be needed, making sure all is in the right place.

And God is just as concerned with every detail about *your* life. He doesn't just keep track of your fingers and toes but the number of hairs on your head! That's how much He values you, how interested He is in every aspect of your being!

Jesus wants you to know you have a Father God who loves you from the tip of your toes to the top of your head. Why? Because you were made in His image. You are His treasured companion and precious daughter. Just as God feeds the birds and tends the flowers, providing for them and helping them to grow, He's there for you, a woman so much more precious than any other creature on the earth.

Lord, I thank You for counting me so worthy of Your love and care.

I know I'm worthy because God values me above all else!

GOD'S GOOD HAND IS UPON YOU

*Upon him was the good hand of his God. For Ezra had
prepared and set his heart to seek the Law of the Lord
[to inquire for it and of it, to require and yearn for it],
and to do. . . . I was strengthened and encouraged,
for the hand of the Lord my God was upon me.*
 EZRA 7:9–10, 28 AMPC

Ezra was a priest who led back to Jerusalem the second wave of Israelites who'd been held captive in Babylon. His journey was successful because "upon him was the good hand of his God"! Why? Because Ezra sought God's Word with all of his heart! But he didn't stop there. He actually lived his life by that Word, gaining the strength and encouragement he needed to lead not only himself but God's people back to the one from whom all good things flow.

That's a good formula for you to follow. Begin taking steps today to prepare your heart, to focus your soul on looking into God's Word. Yearn for it with all your heart, soul, and mind. Then live by its precepts. Doing so will supply you with all the strength and encouragement you need to triumph each day.

---

*I praise You and Your Word, Lord. It's water for my
spiritual thirst and food for my hungry soul.*

I know I'm worthy because God has put His good hand upon me.

GOD GIVES YOU REFUGE UNDER HIS WINGS

"May the LORD repay you for what you have done.
May you be richly rewarded by the LORD, the God of Israel,
under whose wings you have come to take refuge."
RUTH 2:12 NIV

Ruth, raised in the heathen country of Moab, learned of the God of Israel through her husband's family, who'd come to her country during a famine. After she and her mother-in-law, Naomi, were widowed, Naomi decided to return to Israel. Ruth went with her, saying, "Where you go I will go. . . . Your people will be my people and your God my God" (Ruth 1:16 NIV).

Because of her faithfulness to Naomi and her trust in God, Ruth was richly rewarded by finding a godly husband in Boaz and through him birthing Obed, who would become King David's grandfather.

Today, pause and consider under what or whose wings you have taken refuge. Hopefully, you've chosen God's. As cleric Edward Topsell asked, "Who would not forsake the shadow of all the trees in the world to be covered under 'such' wings?"

Make it clear in your mind and heart that if you put your trust in God, you'll be continually under His protection. And He'll reward you for your choice, just as He did Ruth and all His daughters who followed.

Your wings, Lord, are my refuge. I trust in You
to give me the loving shelter I crave. Amen.

I know I'm worthy because God provides me refuge under His wings.

GOD'S WORD HEALS AND RESCUES YOU

He sends forth His word and heals them and
rescues them from the pit and destruction.
PSALM 107:20 AMPC

When King Hezekiah became deathly ill, he prayed to God, reminding Him how he'd been devoted to Him and done good things in His sight. Then God spoke to him through the prophet Isaiah, saying, "I have heard your prayer, I have seen your tears; behold, I will heal you" (2 Kings 20:5 AMPC).

Seven hundred years later, a Roman centurion told Jesus his servant boy "lies in bed, paralyzed and in terrible pain" (Matthew 8:6 NLT). When Jesus told the officer that He would come to his house and heal the boy, the Gentile responded by saying, "Just say the word from where you are, and my servant will be healed" (Matthew 8:8 NLT). When Jesus heard these words, He commended the man for his faith, He sent forth His Word, and the boy was healed.

That promise—that God will send His Word to you to heal you and rescue you—still holds true today. Just believe that your heartfelt prayer will move God. His Word and promises are powerful and proven through the centuries.

I worship You, Lord, and adore Your Word. With each
passing day, increase my faith in the power of my
prayers and Your promises, to Your glory.

I know I'm worthy because God's Word and my prayers surpass all powers.

GOD BREAKS YOUR BONDS

*He brought them out of darkness and the shadow of
death and broke apart the bonds that held them.*
PSALM 107:14 AMPC

So many things can keep you in bondage physically, emotionally, mentally, and spiritually, whether they be addictions, bad habits, dark thoughts, or unseen forces. But you have a God who can break you free from whatever keeps you from living the life to which He has called you.

When the disciple Peter was arrested, imprisoned, and chained, the church prayed for him. That night, while he was sleeping, an angel of the Lord came to him, spoke, and his chains fell off (see Acts 12:7–8). For imprisoned apostles Paul and Silas, who prayed and sang hymns of praise to God, the earth quaked. "All the doors immediately flew open, and the chains of every prisoner fell off!" (Acts 16:26 NLT).

When you're in bondage, pray to God. Praise Him for "His mercy and loving-kindness" (Psalm 107:1 AMPC). Know He will bring you out of the darkness and into the light. He'll break whatever chains are holding you down, because there's no power greater than God's and His love for you.

*Lord, break the chains that have brought me down into the shadows.
Lift me into the light of Your freedom as I pray and praise You.*

I know I'm worthy because my loving God
shakes up heaven and earth to free me.

GOD GRANTS YOU A GOOD NIGHT'S SLEEP

In vain you rise early and stay up late, toiling for food to eat—for he grants sleep to those he loves.
PSALM 127:2 NIV

When you find yourself lying in bed at night, counting sheep instead of catching Z's, it's time to look at what's happening during your daytime hours. Are you anxious about your job or your duties at home? Are you burning the candle at both ends? Are you spending more time chasing money than God? Are you only conscious of God during morning devotions, or are you letting Him into every moment of your day?

When you put all your efforts into God's hands, trusting Him for the results and staying conscious of His presence, you'll find and receive the blessings He's pouring out twenty-four hours a day, seven days a week. That's true no matter what your challenges are.

When God's people were stuck between Pharaoh's chariots and the Red Sea, Moses told them, "The LORD will fight for you; you need only to be still" (Exodus 14:14 NIV). Take these words of wisdom to heart. Rest in God, knowing He'll take care of everything. Be assured He's got you—day and night.

Keep me conscious of Your love and care day and night, Lord. Grant me the sleep of Your peace.

I know I'm worthy because God is taking care of me day and night.

GOD EMBRACES YOU

[I can feel] his left hand under my head
and his right hand embraces me!
SONG OF SOLOMON 2:6 AMPC

Slowly read the words above. Absorb them into your very being. Close your eyes and feel Jesus' left hand under your head. Imagine His right hand embracing you, drawing you to Him with all the love, care, mercy, and joy such a personal relationship with Him provides. Then consider the question posed to you by the Amplified Bible's footnote to these precious words: "Do I have a constant sense of my Shepherd's presence, regardless of my surroundings?"

When stressed, lonely, and heartbroken, during those times when you feel unworthy or fearful, or even when just performing the most mundane task, stop. Go to the one who's waiting with open arms to receive you—just as you are. Go to the source of the love that never dies, that cannot be quenched (see Song of Solomon 8:7).

No matter what's happening in your present, constantly and consistently draw close to the one who whispers, "Arise, my darling, my beautiful one, come with me" (Song of Solomon 2:10 NIV). You'll find yourself at His side, imbued with His overwhelming love.

Oh my Shepherd, I feel Your presence. Thank You for these
words that bring me into the eternal reality of Your love.

I know I'm worthy because when I come to Him,
God embraces me in His all-encompassing love.

GOD SUPPLIES YOU WITH COURAGE

*Do not be afraid of the enemy; [earnestly] remember
the Lord and imprint Him [on your minds], great and
terrible, and [take from Him courage to] fight.*
NEHEMIAH 4:14 AMPC

Nehemiah led the third wave of exiled Israelites back to Jerusalem to rebuild the wall. Unfortunately, neighboring leaders openly objected. They tried to turn the Israelites against their leader and wrote a deceitful letter to the king to get him to override their efforts.

So Nehemiah prayed to God. Nehemiah 4:9 (AMPC) says, "Because of them we made our prayer to our God and set a watch against them day and night." He placed armed guards to protect those rebuilding the wall so their efforts would not be stayed. Then he told the people to take courage.

When others try to impede your efforts to do as God wills, pray to Him. Then remember what He's done in the past. Bring to mind how great and awesome God's power is. Recall how He shook the earth and stilled waters to make a way for His people. Imprint your almighty God, your Father of fathers, on your mind. And take from Him all the courage He's pouring out.

*Lord, I'm imprinting You on my mind. Bring to my remembrance
all You've done for Your sons and daughters. Give me the
courage I need to follow You anywhere and everywhere!*

I know I'm worthy because God supplies all the courage I need.

GOD LOVES YOU

*We know (understand, recognize, are conscious of,
by observation and by experience) and believe (adhere to
and put faith in and rely on) the love God cherishes for us.
God is love, and he who dwells and continues in love dwells
and continues in God, and God dwells and continues in him.*

1 JOHN 4:16 AMPC

The text above expands upon what it means to know and believe you're loved by God. For to know "the love God cherishes for" you is about *understanding* that God loves you so much He sent His only Son to give His life for you. It's about *recognizing* that love when you see it in action in your life or when you read about it in scripture. It's spending the moments of your day *being conscious* of that love, becoming aware of it continually pouring down upon you, by *observing* and *experiencing* its effect in your life.

God truly is love. And your job is to live in that love, to believe in, rely on, and lean into it.

There's nothing more important to God than you. And once you start existing in that reality, only love flows into and out from you. It's a big love. Revel in it. Exude it. And you'll be living in a love that has no end.

Oh God, I praise and thank You for the incomparable love that is You!

I know I'm worthy because my God loves me like no other.

GOD'S WORD GIVES YOU LIGHT

The entrance and unfolding of Your words give light; their unfolding gives understanding (discernment and comprehension) to the simple. . . . Establish my steps and direct them by [means of] Your word; let not any iniquity have dominion over me.

PSALM 119:130, 133 AMPC

• • • • • • • • • • • • • • •

You're blessed because you have one of the greatest sources of power at your fingertips: the Bible—God's Word. But to access that power, you need to open its pages. You need to not just read it but allow it to enter your very being. To unfold itself within you. When you do, you'll find the light that will illuminate your path. You'll see things that were once unclear. You'll find the direction you need to steer clear of those things that will drag you down.

Through Isaiah, God said, "My word. . .will not return to Me empty, without accomplishing what I desire, and without succeeding *in the matter* for which I sent it" (Isaiah 55:11 NASB).

God's Word is here not only to guide you and direct your steps but to mold you into the woman God created you to be. To accomplish what He's sent you to accomplish. For He has deemed you worthy to work with Him for His good end. Allow God and His Word to enter you and light your life.

Thank You, Lord, for the light of Your Word.
May it illuminate me without and within. Amen.

I know I'm worthy because God has blessed me with His Word.

GOD ACHIEVES THE IMPOSSIBLE

The LORD said to Abraham, "Why did Sarah laugh? Why did she say,
'Can an old woman like me have a baby?' Is anything too hard for the
LORD? I will return about this time next year, and Sarah will have a son."
GENESIS 18:13–14 NLT

When Sarah overheard God telling Abraham she would have a son, she laughed in disbelief at the impossibility, the ridiculousness of such a promise. After all, Abraham was nearing one hundred and she, ninety! So she laughed!

But God heard her, so He asked Abraham why she'd laughed, yet God *knew* she doubted He could do the impossible. So God repeated the promise. Then Sarah *denied* she'd laughed! But God called her on it, saying, "No, you did laugh" (Genesis 18:15 NLT).

It's hard to imagine someone that close to the Lord would have the audacity to disbelieve what He says. But the thing is, when you doubt God can do the impossible, *you* are reacting as Sarah did. Laughing at the prospect, denying His promises.

Make it your aim to take another tack. Do not laugh at God, but believe in and smile with assurance in His promises. When you do, you'll see them become your reality.

You are the Lord of the impossible. Help me to put my faith
in Your promises—for my benefit and Your glory!

I know I'm worthy because God does the
impossible—in, with, and through me.

GOD OPENS YOUR EYES

God opened Hagar's eyes, and she saw a well full of water.
She quickly filled her water container and gave the boy a drink.
GENESIS 21:19 NLT

• • • • • • • • • • • • • • • •

After birthing her promised son, Isaac, through Abraham, Sarah told her husband to send the slave Hagar and her son, Ishmael (Abraham's first son), away. Abraham did, and soon Hagar lost her way in the wilderness. When she ran out of water, she and the boy sat down and began to cry.

God sent His angel, who said, "Do not be afraid! God has heard the boy crying as he lies there" (Genesis 21:17 NLT). He then promised to make Ishmael a great nation, and He opened her eyes. It was then she saw the well full of water, filled her bottle, and gave the boy a drink.

When you cry out to God, know that He hears you and that He's waiting for you to tell Him all your troubles. Then keep your ears open to hear His promises. Expect Him to open your eyes to what He has prepared to nourish you—mind, body, heart, spirit, and soul—for the journey. And soon you will find yourself out of the wilderness and into the land of His promises.

Thank You, God, for hearing my cries. Help me keep my ears
open to Your promises and my eyes open to Your provision.

I know I'm worthy because God opens my eyes
to what He has prepared for me.

GOD SUPPLIES ALL YOUR NEEDS

*And this same God who takes care of me will supply all your needs
from his glorious riches, which have been given to us in Christ Jesus.*
PHILIPPIANS 4:19 NLT

• • • • • • • • • • • • • • • • •

When God told Abraham to sacrifice his one and only son through his wife Sarah, Abraham took the boy to Mount Moriah. There, just before Abraham was to kill Isaac, God spoke and stayed his hand. He then knew that Abraham would hold nothing back from Him. When Abraham looked up, he saw a ram caught in a thicket and sacrificed the animal in lieu of Isaac. "Abraham named the place Yahweh-Yireh (which means 'the LORD will provide')" (Genesis 22:14 NLT).

Thousands of years later, God would provide Jesus, the Lamb of God, to be sacrificed once to make peace for all with God.

The word *provision* comes from the Latin, meaning "a foreseeing" or "to look ahead." The fact that God provides all you need means He is continually looking ahead, seeing what you'll need before you need it, and readying your supply.

Rest easy in that knowledge. Know that in Christ you will never lack. Do not doubt that your loving God is always way ahead of you, preparing your supply before you even know you need it.

---

*Yahweh-Yireh, I love that You're constantly preparing what I'll need.
Such love makes me truly thankful to You, the source of my supply.*

I know I'm worthy because God supplies all my needs.

GOD COMFORTS, ENCOURAGES, REFRESHES, AND CHEERS YOU

God. . .comforts and encourages and refreshes
and cheers the depressed and the sinking.
2 CORINTHIANS 7:6 AMPC

Where do you go when you need comfort? Who do you look for when you need encouragement? What refreshes your spirit? Who cheers you when you're sad? What do you reach out for or whom do you cling to when you feel you are sinking down into the abyss?

Do you eat chocolate cake, binge a favorite TV show, refresh yourself with caffeine, or reach out for something that's only a temporary fix at best?

For a true remedy, there's only one place to go: God. Dig into Him and His Word. There you'll find the comfort that dries your eyes, the encouragement that helps you persevere, the water that refreshes, the cheer that reinvigorates, and the hope that lifts you up.

Once you're fortified by God's Word, what follows on its heels is God's doing, according to His providence. To Paul, who wrote today's verse, God sent his friend Titus. To you, God may send a warm breeze, prompt a friend's phone call, or reveal a loved one's smile. Only God can turn your pain into joy.

God, when I need comfort, encouragement, and cheering, lead me into Your Word. I'll then watch for Your providence to raise me even further!

I know I'm worthy because God, His Word, and His providence comfort me like no other.

GOD GIFTS ME WITH HIS PEACE

Peace I leave with you; My [own] peace I now give and bequeath to you. Not as the world gives do I give to you. Do not let your hearts be troubled, neither let them be afraid. [Stop allowing yourselves to be agitated and disturbed; and do not permit yourselves to be fearful and intimidated and cowardly and unsettled.]
JOHN 14:27 AMPC

Jesus has left you with His peace. His peace is not the peace of an unbelieving world, which brings no lasting good or real prosperity. It's the inner peace of which He is your only source. All you have to do is not doubt that this peace is available to you. You need simply to take it up!

Jesus adds to the statement about His gift of peace by telling you to *stop allowing* yourself to be troubled, frustrated, perturbed, and disturbed. *Do not let yourself* live in fear, be intimidated, be afraid of your own shadow, or be anxious.

But how do you gain such peace? By having and being conscious of an unbroken and loving relationship between Him and you.

Accept the gift that keeps on giving. Take up the peace only Jesus can provide. "And the peace of God, which transcends all understanding, will guard your hearts and your minds in Christ Jesus" (Philippians 4:7 NIV).

I revel in the gift of Your peace, Jesus.
Your very own peace has become mine.

I know I'm worthy because Jesus gives me peace beyond understanding.

GOD GIVES YOU SUCCESS

He said to me, The Lord, in Whose presence I walk [habitually],
will send His Angel with you and prosper your way.
GENESIS 24:40 AMPC

Abraham didn't want his son to marry a woman from among the Canaanites where he'd settled. So he sent his servant to find a wife for Isaac among his own people. Before the servant left, Abraham told him God "will send His Angel before you, and you will take a wife from there for my son" (Genesis 24:7 AMPC).

The obedient and faithful servant went on his way. When he reached Abraham's relatives, he got down on his knees and said, "I pray You, cause me to meet with good success today" (Genesis 24:12 AMPC). He asked for God to indicate which girl He had selected to be Isaac's wife. When he saw Rebekah, he watched and waited to see what God would reveal. When he realized she was the one God had appointed, he bowed down and worshipped the Lord (see Genesis 24:26).

When you're obedient to God, when you consistently walk in His presence, when you pause to pray to and praise Him, He will send His angel before you and prosper you on your way. What are you waiting for?

Lord, help me to walk with You in every aspect of
my journey, to obediently follow wherever You lead.

I know I'm worthy because as I walk with God, He grants me success.

41

GOD WANTS YOU TO ABIDE IN HIM

Dwell in Me, and I will dwell in you. [Live in Me, and I will live in you.]. . . I am the Vine; you are the branches. Whoever lives in Me and I in him bears much (abundant) fruit. However, apart from Me [cut off from vital union with Me] you can do nothing.
JOHN 15:4–5 AMPC

Jesus chose you to produce fruit that lasts, "so that the Father will give you whatever you ask for" (John 15:16 NLT), using His name. But to be productive, you must have a vital union with Jesus. Without Him, "you can do nothing."

Just as a branch cut off from the vine cannot grow or stand without the sap the vine provides, you, without living a life with Jesus, will have no strength to do what He's purposed you to do. Thus, you need to abide in Jesus, the Vine. Be united with Him by living a life of faith, dependent on Him alone, true to His commandments, and following His example.

As you live in Jesus, He will live in you. And there's no telling what you'll accomplish as you stay connected with the one who walks on water.

Help me abide in You, Jesus, and bear the fruit You've purposed me to bear for You.

I know I'm worthy because I live in God and He in me.

GOD GRANTS YOUR REQUESTS

*"If you abide in Me, and My words abide in you,
ask whatever you wish, and it will be done for you."*
JOHN 15:7 NASB

Jesus gives you two provisions to answered prayer. The first is to abide in Him, which means to have a vital union with Him, to live a life of faith following His example and His command to love God and love others as yourself (see Mark 12:30-31). The second is for Jesus' words to abide in you. When His words are living, at home, abiding within you, your thoughts will be transformed. They will become the thoughts that follow Jesus' lines of thinking. As you dwell in Him and His words dwell in you, you will begin to desire what God desires. You will be in alignment with His will. You will pray according to His words. And so your prayers will please Him.

As you plant more and more of Jesus' words within your soul, mind, and spirit, His will and way will begin to take root. You and your prayers will produce more fruit. You will be living more and more for God and His kingdom to His glory (see John 15:8).

---

*Jesus, may my desires become Yours as I abide in
You and Your words in me. To God's glory. Amen.*

I know I'm worthy because as I dwell in Jesus,
and His words in me, God grants my requests.

GOD HAS A PLACE FOR YOU

*"My Father's house has many rooms; if that were not so, would I
have told you that I am going there to prepare a place for you?
And if I go and prepare a place for you, I will come back and
take you to be with me that you also may be where I am."*
JOHN 14:2-3 NIV

Jesus has already gone ahead and prepared a place—just for you—in God's house.

Some scholars say God's house refers to heaven, that someday Jesus will return and take us all back with Him. Yet others think God's house refers to our dwelling place being with God now on earth and later in the heavenlies. That we attain that prepared place by loving Him and keeping His commandments. They base this idea on the following:

> *All praise to God, the Father of our Lord Jesus Christ, who
> has blessed us with every spiritual blessing in the heavenly
> realms because we are united with Christ.* Ephesians 1:3 NLT

> *For he raised us from the dead along with Christ and
> seated us with him in the heavenly realms because we are
> united with Christ Jesus.* Ephesians 2:6 NLT

Regardless of how you view today's verses, you can revel in the fact that God loves you so much He wants *you* to be with *Him*—forever and ever!

Lord, thank You for providing a place for me with You. What love!

I know I'm worthy because God wants me with Him forever.

GOD DIRECTS YOU

He will surely be gracious to you at the sound of your cry;
when He hears it, He will answer you. . . . And your ears will
hear a word behind you, saying, This is the way; walk in it,
when you turn to the right hand and when you turn to the left.
ISAIAH 30:19, 21 AMPC

Have you ever felt lost when you're on a road trip, even when you have a GPS? The good news is that, as a believer, you never need to feel lost on your spiritual journey. That's because God is your navigator. When He hears you cry out, He will answer you directly. If you obey Him, seek His wisdom, look for and expect His directions, you'll hear a voice, a whisper telling you, "Go this way. Walk in the path I have laid out before you. I am here to tell you whether you should go right or turn left."

Today and every day, go to God and ask Him, "What would you have me do and say today, Lord? What are my next steps? Which path would you have me take?" Then listen quietly for His whisper. Remain sensitive to the Holy Spirit's guidance, and obey His directions. When you do, you'll be on the right path!

What steps would You like me to take today, Lord? I'm listening.

I know I'm worthy because God directs my
every step as I walk closer to Him.

GOD GIVES YOU THE KEY TO JOY

"When you obey my commandments, you remain in my love, just as I obey my Father's commandments and remain in his love. I have told you these things so that you will be filled with my joy. Yes, your joy will overflow!"
JOHN 15:10-11 NLT

• • • • • • • • • • • • • •

Jesus says that if you obey His commandments—loving God with all your heart, soul, strength, and mind, and loving others as you love yourself—and follow His path, you'll be living in His love. That higher love knows no bounds and is yours for the taking. And when you do, you'll be overflowing with joy!

Jesus obeyed His Father, God, while He was here on the earth. To Him, doing so was not hard work or menial labor. It was a pleasure, an opportunity to glorify His Father, to allow God's amazing love and power to flow through Him and spill over onto others.

If you're looking for joy—a deep-down happiness that's not dependent on outward circumstances—follow God's commandments, Jesus' example, and the Holy Spirit's promptings. Then you'll be on your way to obtaining and remaining in the spiritual love and joy that never ends!

Lord, help me to remain in Your Word, to obey Your commands, to live my life as Jesus did, and to follow the Spirit's promptings so that I may have the joy that overflows!

I know I'm worthy because God has given me the key to obtaining His joy.

GOD ESTABLISHES YOUR WORK

*And let the beauty and delightfulness and favor of the Lord
our God be upon us; confirm and establish the work of our
hands—yes, the work of our hands, confirm and establish it.*
PSALM 90:17 AMPC

When God gave Moses the instructions on how He wanted His house (the tabernacle) built, He named two men—Bezalel and Oholiab—as those whom He'd personally chosen and called to be His craftsmen for the project. He filled them with the "Spirit of God, with wisdom, with understanding, with knowledge and with all kinds of skills" (Exodus 31:3 NIV).

God does the same for you! He's uniquely gifted you not just with His Spirit but with all the talent and resources you need to work out your calling!

Today, if you're looking for career advice or how to serve in God's house, pray for God to confirm and establish your work. Ask Him to reveal the talents He wants you to expend on His behalf. You've been made in the image of your Master Creator. Answer His call so that you can become His cocreator as you build upon His beauty in this world.

---

*Reveal to me, Lord, what talents You would have me put my
hands to for You. Establish my work so I may answer Your call.*

I know I'm worthy because God has called me and
equipped me with skills to use for Him in this world.

GOD IS YOUR PERSONAL BRAVERY

The Lord God is my Strength, my personal bravery, and my invincible army; He makes my feet like hinds' feet and will make me to walk [not to stand still in terror, but to walk] and make [spiritual] progress upon my high places [of trouble, suffering, or responsibility]!
HABAKKUK 3:19 AMPC

When things are going well, it's easy to be courageous, to have an upbeat attitude, to feel secure and have hope. But when things start going wrong or something unexpected and unwanted happens, when you are shaken to the core, that's when you and your faith are tested.

God wants you to base your safety and hope not on blessings that are temporary at best but on God Himself (see Habakkuk 2:4). When you do, He will become your strength, your personal army that can never be defeated. He will always protect you and never retreat. With God in you and on your side, you will not be frozen like a deer in the headlights, find yourself on the run, or be shaking in your boots. Instead He will be the strength that empowers you to walk strong. He will lead you to the mountaintop of victory.

Be my strength and my power, Lord. Be my personal bodyguard. With You in my heart, mind, spirit, and soul, I know I can face anything—during good times and bad!

I know I'm worthy because the King of the universe is my courage, security, hope, and strength!

GOD IS FAITHFUL TO YOU

So the LORD must wait for you to come to him so he can show you his love and compassion. For the LORD is a faithful God. Blessed are those who wait for his help.

ISAIAH 30:18 NLT

God promised Abraham that he would be the father of many nations (see Genesis 12:1–3). But for years, Abraham and his wife, Sarah, remained childless. Yet God continued to remind Abraham he would have many descendants (see Genesis 13:16; 15:1–6; 17:6–7; 18:10).

At one point, Sarah ran out of patience, telling Abraham to have a child by her maid, Hagar. But that's not the son God had promised or planned for Abraham (see Genesis 16). It was only when Abraham was one hundred years old and Sarah was ninety that the God-promised and God-intended son was born (see Genesis 21:1–5).

Hebrews 6:15 (NLT) says, "Abraham waited patiently, and he received what God had promised." God wants you to have that same patience.

Are you waiting for God to work in a certain situation in your life? Are you waiting for Him to come through on His promises? If so, wait for Him. He's working behind the scenes to bring about a blessing for you.

Lord, I know You are a faithful God, true to all Your promises. You love me and have compassion on me. I take strength in this and await Your blessings!

I know I'm worthy because my loving and compassionate God is faithful to me!

GOD IS YOUR HELP

I lift up my eyes to the mountains—where does my help come from?
My help comes from the LORD, the Maker of heaven and earth.
He will not let your foot slip—he who watches over you will not slumber.
PSALM 121:1-3 NIV

When you need help, where or to whom or to what do you look? Isaiah warned against God's people looking to the power of men for help instead of to God. He wrote: "Woe to those who go down to Egypt for help, who rely on horses, who trust in the multitude of their chariots and in the great strength of their horsemen, but do not look to the Holy One of Israel, or seek help from the LORD" (Isaiah 31:1 NIV). Why? Because when they look to men's strength and power, disaster is sure to come!

Look to God as the true source of your help. He—the Creator of heaven and earth—is watching over you day and night. When you're sleeping, His eyes are wide open as He keeps watch. He "will keep you from all harm—he will watch over your life. . .over your coming and going both now and forevermore" (Psalm 121:7-8 NIV)!

Keep that in mind as you step in and out the door—today and every day!

I'm looking to You alone for my help, Lord!

I know I'm worthy because God, my help, is constantly watching over me!

GOD REVEALS HIMSELF TO YOU

I have made Your Name known to them and revealed Your
character and Your very Self, and I will continue to make [You]
known, that the love which You have bestowed upon Me may be
in them [felt in their hearts] and that I [Myself] may be in them.
JOHN 17:26 AMPC

Do you sometimes wonder who God really is, what He's like? To discover who
your Lord and Creator is, look at Jesus. For He says, "Anyone who has seen
Me has seen the Father" (John 14:9 AMPC).

Consider Jesus' love, how He heals, frees, teaches, and has compassion
on all those He encounters. How He has not left you alone but has gifted you
with the Holy Spirit, through whom He continues to nurture and care for
you. How all this was done to show you who He and God are—love personified.

As you pray today, reflect upon the love that God showed for His one and
only Son. Feel that love of God in your heart. Jesus and the Spirit will help.
All you need to do is receive them and abide in the treasure of their love.

I come to You today, Lord, with a heart ready and willing
to receive Your love that I may know You even more.

I know I'm worthy because God has revealed Himself
to me and poured His love into my heart.

GOD GIVES YOU ACCESS TO HIS HIGHER MIND

"For My thoughts are not your thoughts, nor are your ways My ways,"
declares the LORD. "For as the heavens are higher than the earth, so are
My ways higher than your ways and My thoughts than your thoughts."
ISAIAH 55:8–9 NASB

Proverbs 23:7 says that whatever you're thinking within your heart makes you who you are. If your thoughts are negative, you'll be negative. If your thoughts are loving, you'll be loving. In other words, your thoughts have great sway over you, prompting you to actually do and be without what you're thinking within.

God says His thoughts and ways are not your thoughts and ways. That's because His are so much higher than yours! So what's a woman to do? Rely on God's wisdom instead of your own to exchange your thoughts for His.

You don't need to understand His thoughts, His plans, His will, His words. Just obey them, even if they seem beyond your reasoning. Trust that He knows what He's doing, that He has something good in mind for you. His perspective is so much greater than your own. And His way is the best way.

Lord, sometimes my thoughts lead me astray. Help me
replace my thoughts with Your words, and help me to
do and be what You would have me do and be.

I know I'm worthy because through His Word,
God gives me access to His higher mind.

GOD GUIDES YOU DAY AND NIGHT

*GOD went ahead of them in a Pillar of Cloud during the
day to guide them on the way, and at night in a Pillar of
Fire to give them light.... The Pillar of Cloud by day and
the Pillar of Fire by night never left the people.*
EXODUS 13:21–22 MSG

When God's people were in bondage and cried out to Him for help, He literally plagued the Egyptians who enslaved them. When Pharaoh finally let the Israelites go, "God didn't lead them by the road through the land of the Philistines, which was the shortest route, for God thought, 'If the people encounter war, they'll change their minds and go back to Egypt' " (Exodus 13:17 MSG). So He led them through the wilderness. And as His people traveled, God never left them. He guided them day and night toward the Red Sea, which He eventually parted so the people could walk through on dry land.

God's guiding you the same way. He knows your strengths and your weaknesses. He knows how to guide you along the best route, even if it seems to you the long way around. And He will remove any obstacles in your path. With God, you're never lost in the dark but are continually guided by His loving presence.

*With You, Lord, I'm never lost. Thank You
for Your continual guidance down every road.*

I know I'm worthy because God guides me day and night.

GOD ENCOURAGES AND STRENGTHENS YOU

*David was greatly distressed, for the men spoke of stoning
him because the souls of them all were bitterly grieved,
each man for his sons and daughters. But David encouraged
and strengthened himself in the Lord his God.*

1 SAMUEL 30:6 AMPC

While David and his men were away at war, the Amalekites made a raid on
their village. They'd not only burned it down but took captive all the town's
wives and children. When David and his men came home, they wept until
they had no more tears to shed. Then the men talked of stoning David.

"But David encouraged *and* strengthened himself in the Lord his God"
through prayer. And God told him what to do: "Pursue, for you shall surely
overtake them and without fail recover all" (1 Samuel 30:8 AMPC). David
followed God's instructions and recovered not only all the townspeople but
their enemy's livestock as well.

There will be times of adversity during which the best and only place to
turn will be to God through prayer. He's the greatest source of encouragement
and strength you'll need. With His help, you'll find yourself recovering all
that's been taken—and so much more!

*I'm encouraged and strengthened just by being in Your
presence, Lord. Thank You for always being there in the darkest
moments of my life and leading me to ultimate victory!*

I know I'm worthy because God's presence
blesses me with strength and encouragement.

GOD'S SPIRIT PRAYS FOR YOU

*We don't know what God wants us to pray for. But the Holy Spirit
prays for us with groanings that cannot be expressed in words.
And the Father who knows all hearts knows what the Spirit is saying,
for the Spirit pleads for us believers in harmony with God's own will.*
ROMANS 8:26–27 NLT

• • • • • • • • • • • • • •

At times situations can be so complicated that you might not know exactly how to pray about it. Or your heart is so wounded that you cannot find the words to say to God. The wonder of all this is that God has given you the Holy Spirit. He will pray for you for those things that you cannot express in words. He will translate your moans, groans, and sighs to God. And the Father, who knows your heart like no other, will understand what the Spirit is saying.

And there's more! The Spirit will then guide you into God's Word, showing you what you need to know and giving you the power to apply that wisdom to your life—keeping you in the blessed harmony with God and what He has planned for you!

So don't be afraid to pray. Don't throw up your hands when you cannot find the words. Just tap into the presence and power of the Holy Spirit. He'll lead you within and without.

---

*Thank You, Spirit, for always being there for me,
being my translator, comforter, and guide.*

I know I'm worthy because God's Spirit prays for me.

GOD STICKS WITH YOU

"I am with you, and I will protect you wherever you go. One day I will bring you back to this land. I will not leave you until I have finished giving you everything I have promised you." Then Jacob awoke from his sleep and said, "Surely the LORD is in this place, and I wasn't even aware of it!"

GENESIS 28:15–16 NLT

Having deceived his brother and father, Jacob was on the run. His first night away from home, he slept under the stars, using a rock as a pillow. He dreamed of a ladder between heaven and earth. God stood at the top as His angels ascended and descended upon it.

Toward the end of his dream, Jacob heard God's promise that He'd always be with him, protecting him and never leaving him until Jacob had received all God promised him. When Jacob woke, he was amazed. God was where he was, and Jacob didn't even realize it!

No matter what you're going through—whether or not the circumstances are of your own making—God is with you. Even during the hardest trials, He's looking out for you, protecting you, sticking with you until all His promises to you are fulfilled. You don't need to wonder. God will never leave you!

Lord, thank You for sticking with me through thick and thin. Help me to be continually aware of Your presence at my side!

I know I'm worthy because God sticks with me no matter what.

GOD BREAKS THROUGH FOR YOU

So [Israel] came up to Baal-perazim, and David smote [the
Philistines] there. Then David said, God has broken my enemies by
my hand, like the bursting forth of waters. Therefore they called
the name of that place Baal-perazim [Lord of breaking through].
1 CHRONICLES 14:11 AMPC

Are you seeking a breakthrough in some area of your life? If so, are you attempting to do it in your own power and wisdom?

When the Philistines heard that David had been anointed king over Israel, they decided to challenge him. David's first response was to ask the Lord if he should go up against them and, if he did, would God give them into his hand. God told David to go. He would give him victory. David followed God's instructions. When he was victorious, he said God had broken through his enemies and so named the place Baal-perazim, which means "Lord of breaking through."

Because David earnestly sought God, listened to Him, then followed His guidance, God gave him many breakthroughs. When you're looking for a breakthrough, instead of attempting to achieve one in your own power and wisdom, seek God. Listen to what He has to say, and then follow His wisdom, being patient for Him to work things out His way.

Lord, I need a breakthrough, so I'm seeking Your face,
listening for Your guidance, ready to obey.

I know I'm worthy because God breaks through barriers for me.

GOD PROSPERS THE WORK OF YOUR HANDS

But the Lord was with Joseph, and he [though a slave]
was a successful and prosperous man. . . . And his master
saw that the Lord was with him and that the Lord made
all that he did to flourish and succeed in his hand.

GENESIS 39:2–3 AMPC

Joseph had a rough span of about twelve years. First his jealous brothers stuck him in a pit, and then they sold him to traders. He landed as a slave to an Egyptian and was imprisoned based on false accusations from his master's wife.

Yet here's the thing: No matter what happened to him, Joseph never blamed God for his circumstances. As hard as his trials were, away from his home and loving father, Joseph never stopped trusting that God would help him. He patiently awaited better days and continued to serve the Lord from wherever he landed. Because of all these things, God prospered whatever Joseph put his hand to—and people noticed!

Whatever work came to Joseph, he did it the best that he could, trusting God to give him wisdom and guidance where needed. As his work blessed others, Joseph himself was blessed. As you do the same, God will prosper you and those whose lives you touch! It's a win-win!

I'm trusting You, Lord, to help me do
the best work I can—for You and others!

I know I'm worthy because God prospers the work of my hands.

GOD IS IN CONTROL OF YOUR CIRCUMSTANCES

So it was God who sent me here, not you! . . . You intended to harm me, but God intended it all for good. He brought me to this position so I could save the lives of many people.
GENESIS 45:8; 50:20 NLT

• • • • • • • • • • • • • • • •

No matter what happened to Joseph—abandoned, sold into slavery, sent to a dungeon, forgotten—He knew God was in control of his circumstances. And Joseph trusted God every day while learning valuable lessons every step of the way. One day, he was sent to interpret Pharaoh's dreams. The leader of Egypt, impressed with Joseph, made him lord of his household and ruler over the land.

It was his high-ranking position in Egypt that enabled Joseph to be able to save the lives of his father and his brothers' families. And it was his trust that God was in control all the time that allowed him to forgive them. Joseph realized that it was actually God who had worked this plan!

Rest easy. Know God is in control. He will make all things work for good if you will just trust Him, be patient, and never lose your faith.

What a relief, Lord, to know You are always working out my circumstance for good. Thank You for always being with me!

I know I'm worthy because God will work all for good.

GOD PROVIDES YOUR "NEVERTHELESS"

The king and his men marched to Jerusalem to attack the Jebusites, who lived there. The Jebusites said to David, "You will not get in here; even the blind and the lame can ward you off." They thought, "David cannot get in here." Nevertheless, David captured the fortress of Zion—which is the City of David.
2 SAMUEL 5:6–7 NIV

When David became king over all Israel, he and his men marched to Jerusalem to attack the people who lived there. But the inhabitants taunted David, disparaging his strength and vowing he would never be able to even get into the city. But because David walked closely with, consulted with, and obeyed God, he did indeed capture the city and made it his stronghold from which he would rule over God's people. "And he became more and more powerful, because the LORD God Almighty was with him" (2 Samuel 5:10 NIV).

When you walk closely with God, asking for His guidance at every crossroad and following Him with all your heart as did David, you too can count on God providing you with a "nevertheless," no matter how daunting the challenge. Nothing is impossible with God!

I want to walk so closely with You, Lord, that I no longer know where I end and You begin. With You I know no challenge can stand in our way!

I know I'm worthy because God meets
my challenges with a "nevertheless."

GOD GIVES YOU ASSURANCE TO GO FORWARD

She said, "It will be well." Then she saddled a donkey and said to her servant, "Drive and go forward; do not slow down."
2 KINGS 4:23–24 NASB

A childless Shunammite woman made a room in her house for the prophet Elijah to stay in whenever he came to town. In return for her hospitality, Elijah said she'd have a son the coming spring. And she did! But several years later, that son suffered a headache and died in her arms. After laying him on Elijah's bed, she told her husband she was going to see the man of God. He asked her why now. She replied, "It will be well," then rode off to find Elijah.

Seeing her coming, Elijah told his servant, Gehazi, to run and meet her and ask if all was well. She answered, "It is well" (2 Kings 4:26 NASB). But when she came face-to-face with Elijah, she, in obvious distress, held his feet, saying, "Did I ask for a son from my lord?" (v. 28). Eventually, Elijah raised the boy from the dead and returned him to his mother's arms.

This Shunammite woman remained calm because she knew that with God all would be well. May you move forward with such positive faith no matter what life brings. When you do, miracles await.

With You, God, I know all will be well.

I know I'm worthy because God gives me the assurance to move forward.

GOD REWARDS YOUR PATIENCE

To You I lift up my eyes, O You who are enthroned in the heavens!
Behold, as the eyes of servants look to the hand of their master,
as the eyes of a maid to the hand of her mistress, so our eyes
look to the LORD our God, until He is gracious to us.
PSALM 123:1–2 NASB

You've prayed and prayed, and still God hasn't answered your plea for help and kindness. But, in reality, He *has*! He's behind the scenes, working things out on your behalf, setting the stage, getting all ready and into place.

Be assured God has a better plan than you could ever imagine. He knows something you don't, and time needs to pass before you actually receive the blessings awaiting you. Your job is to keep looking to Him, knowing you'll see His answer.

Meanwhile, be patient. Don't make the mistake of running ahead of God or taking matters into your own hands. That's what Sarah did, and she ended up messing up not only her own life but those of others (see Genesis 16 and 21).

Continue looking to God, your Lord and master. He is and will forever be gracious. Keep your faith and your focus on Him, knowing that with Him all will turn out well.

Thank You, Lord, for Your love, grace, and kindness.
Build up my patience and peace as I keep my eyes on You.

I know I'm worthy because God rewards
me as I patiently look to Him for help.

GOD'S POWER HEALS YOU

*Immediately her flow of blood was dried up at the source, and [suddenly]
she felt in her body that she was healed. . . . And Jesus, recognizing in
Himself that the power proceeding from Him had gone forth, turned
around immediately in the crowd and said, Who touched My clothes?*

MARK 5:29–30 AMPC

A woman who'd been hemorrhaging for twelve years had spent all her money
on doctors but was still not healed. She heard about Jesus, so she came up
to Him amid the crowd and touched His garment. She kept saying to herself,
"If I only touch His garments, I shall be restored to health" (Mark 5:28 AMPC).
And immediately, Jesus' power entered her body and she was healed!

When she finally admitted to Jesus that it was she who'd touched Him, He
said, "Daughter, your faith (your trust and confidence in Me, springing from
faith in God) has restored you to health. Go in (into) peace and be continually
healed *and* freed from your [distressing bodily] disease" (Mark 5:34 AMPC).

God has the power to heal. Yet you must have faith in that power when
you reach out to Him. For it is that faith that will heal you, save you, and give
you peace.

*I believe You can heal me, Lord. You can restore me
physically, mentally, and spiritually. So I reach out
for You in this moment, awaiting Your power.*

I know I'm worthy because God's power heals me.

GOD QUIETS YOUR HEART

Let be and be still, and know (recognize and understand) that I am God.
PSALM 46:10 AMPC

God wants you to be still. To be relaxed, to let your hands go limp. Do not make any effort, but instead leave all things in God's hands and have no more anxiety over whatever has come against you. Just let things be. Let yourself grow still, calm, and quiet. Recognize that God has you.

To obtain that quietness of heart, mind, soul, spirit, and body, you must believe that God is your refuge and strength (see Psalm 46:1 AMPC). He has proven His help in times of trouble. So you need not fear, "though the earth should change and though the mountains be shaken into the midst of the seas, though its waters roar and foam, though the mountains tremble at its swelling *and* tumult" (Psalm 46:2–3 AMPC). God is your high tower (see Psalm 46:7 AMPC), the place you can go to rise above all fears and anxieties and simply rest in the one who holds the whole world in His hands and loves you like no other.

---

*Lord, I come to You, relaxed in body. With You in my life,
I know I am safe, secure, and dearly loved. You alone help
me to rise above the fray and find a peace like no other.*

I know I'm worthy because God, my high tower
and strength, comes and quiets my heart.

GOD LEADS YOU TO TRIUMPH

The wall was finished. . . . It had taken fifty-two days.
When all our enemies heard the news and all the
surrounding nations saw it, our enemies totally lost their
nerve. They knew that God was behind this work.
NEHEMIAH 6:15–16 MSG

Nehemiah had come up against a lot of challenges when he and the once-exiled Jews were building the wall around Jerusalem. Enemy leaders plotted to harm Nehemiah, trying to get him to stop the work and come see them. Five times they sent him a message, trying to intimidate him, to discourage the workers, to undermine their determination. But instead of giving in to discouragement or fear, Nehemiah prayed to God, "Give me strength" (Nehemiah 6:9 MSG). And the wall was completed in fifty-two days because God was behind all the efforts of His people!

God is behind all your efforts as well. No matter how many people plot to discourage you, pray to God for strength. Don't let any setbacks, obstacles, or disappointments keep you from doing what God has called you to do. Choose to see things through, for God is behind your work and will help you accomplish it!

Thank You, Lord, for Your words of encouragement and Your
strength to complete all You have set my hands to do!

I know I'm worthy because my God leads me to victory!

THE JOY OF GOD IS YOUR STRENGTH

*Then [Ezra] told them, Go your way, eat the fat, drink the sweet
drink, and send portions to him for whom nothing is prepared;
for this day is holy to our Lord. And be not grieved and depressed,
for the joy of the Lord is your strength and stronghold.*
NEHEMIAH 8:10 AMPC

After Jerusalem's wall was completed, Ezra read to the Jews the book of the
law of Moses. When the people had realized how much they had strayed from
God, they began to weep and moan. But Ezra told them to not be depressed
but to be full of joy because the joy of the Lord—their God who was full of
forgiveness, compassion, and grace; slow to anger; abounding in love (see
Nehemiah 9:17)—was their strength! He was their stronghold!

The apostle Paul built on this when he told Christ-followers to "be
happy [in your faith] *and* rejoice *and* be glad-hearted continually (always)"
(1 Thessalonians 5:16 AMPC)! When you have joy in God and all He's done
for you, you will have the strength and be fortified, energized, and enabled
to do what He's already equipped you to do!

*Lord, help me find the path to joy that my relationship with You provides.
Overflow me with Your love and forgiveness, Your strength and
encouragement. In You I find all the joy I could ever desire—and more!*

**I know I'm worthy because my joy in the Lord
is where I find all the strength I need!**

GOD COMMANDS YOU TO KEEP FAITH

*Overhearing but ignoring what they said, Jesus said to
the ruler of the synagogue, Do not be seized with alarm
and struck with fear; only keep on believing.*
MARK 5:36 AMPC

Jairus, a leader of a synagogue, fell at Jesus' feet and begged Jesus to come lay His hands on his daughter, who was near death. As Jesus began walking off with Jairus, His garment was touched by a woman with an issue of blood. Jesus' power healed her instantly. While Jesus was saying to the woman, "Daughter, your faith has made you well. Go in peace" (Mark 5:34 NLT), some people came and told Jairus that his daughter had died and asked why he continued to bother Jesus.

When Jesus overheard them, He ignored what they said and told Jairus, "Do not be seized with alarm *and* struck with fear; only keep on believing."

When Jesus arrived at the house where people were weeping and wailing, He told them to stop, that Jairus's daughter was not dead but sleeping. After they laughed at Him, Jesus sent them out, and then He took the child's hand and told her to get up—and she did!

When your faith prompts you to go to Jesus, don't be discouraged by mockers, laughers, or discouragers. Follow Jesus' command to stay calm and keep believing. Jesus will work a miracle for you!

You do the impossible, Lord. I believe in You!

I know I'm worthy because God works miracles
when I follow His command to keep on believing!

GOD POURS ABUNDANT BLESSINGS UPON YOU

And God is able to bless you abundantly, so that in all things at all times, having all that you need, you will abound in every good work.
2 CORINTHIANS 9:8 NIV

"Whoever sows sparingly will also reap sparingly, and whoever sows generously will also reap generously" (2 Corinthians 9:6 NIV) is a spiritual law at work in your life and in the world. With God, the more you give—the more seeds you liberally scatter without regard or anxiety as to where they'll land—the more you'll reap!

And as you continue to give of yourself and your resources to help others and to serve God, He will continue to make sure you have *more* than you need! Once you grasp this concept and test it, you'll realize its truth. You'll become the eager, generous, and joyful giver God created you to be.

Today, pray to God. Then have a "heart" talk with yourself, deciding what you want to give—in terms of not just your money but your talents, resources, and time. Fix it firm in your mind that God will resupply whatever you expend. Then you will become a lovely conduit through whom His heavenly blessings will flow out onto the earth.

Make me Your conduit of blessings, Lord!
Show me what I am to do. I'm ready to give!

I know I'm worthy because God continually
pours His blessing upon me as I sow for Him!

GOD HELPS YOU OVERCOME THE DOUBT IN YOUR HEART

Jesus said, "If? There are no 'ifs' among believers.
Anything can happen." . . . The father cried,
"Then I believe. Help me with my doubts!"
MARK 9:23–24 MSG

A man came to Jesus with his son who had fits that exposed him to danger. The disciples had been unable to help. So the father said to Jesus, "If you can do anything, do it. Have a heart and help us!" (Mark 9:22 MSG). Jesus replied, "If? There are no 'ifs' among believers. Anything can happen." And the man replied, "Then I believe. Help me with my doubts!" Within minutes, Jesus rid the boy of the spirit and helped him stand.

You may have had occasions when you wondered if Jesus could do the impossible. When that happens, go to Jesus. Admit you need Him to help you overcome the doubts in your heart. Ask Him for the faith to believe He can do the impossible. Know that although you don't see any way forward, He does. As you do, you'll see your faith grow and your doubts fade as He works the impossible in His time and way. What else would He do for a woman He loves?

I believe, Lord. Help me with my unbelief!

I know I'm worthy because God helps me overcome all doubts in my heart!

GOD WORKS ALL THINGS FOR GOOD

We know that God causes everything to work together for the good of those who love God and are called according to his purpose for them.
ROMANS 8:28 NLT

Sometimes bad things happen to good people. Consider Lazarus. He lived in Bethany with his sisters, Mary and Martha. When Lazarus was ill, the sisters sent word to Jesus. But Jesus said Lazarus' illness wouldn't end in death, and God's glory would be revealed. Then Jesus stayed where He was for two more days before He began making His way to Bethany. By the time He arrived, Lazarus had been dead four days.

Martha and Mary both told Jesus that if He'd been there, Lazarus wouldn't have died, though Martha added that even now God would give Jesus whatever He asked.

On His way to Lazarus' resting place, Jesus wept. On His arrival, He yelled, "Lazarus, come out!" (John 11:43 NLT), and he did. And all who believed saw God's glory!

God has called you for a purpose. He has a plan for your life. Although you may not understand on this side of heaven why something has happened, you can be assured God is working things together for your good. Believe in Him, trust in His ways, and you too will see God's glory.

Lord, I know You have a plan to work all things for good. Help me to trust in this truth.

I know I'm worthy because God works all things for my good!

GOD RE-CREATED YOU FOR GOOD WORKS

We are God's [own] handiwork (His workmanship), recreated in Christ Jesus, [born anew] that we may do those good works which God predestined (planned beforehand) for us [taking paths which He prepared ahead of time], that we should walk in them [living the good life which He prearranged and made ready for us to live].
EPHESIANS 2:10 AMPC

God made every little bit of you—your eyebrows, toes, fingernails, heart, personality, emotions, everything! Then, when you accepted Jesus, you were re-created, reformed, so you could do all God had planned for you since the beginning of time!

Imagine that! God has had you in and on His mind since before the world or you were created. He's already figured out what paths you are to take, and He's prepared your way down them. He's prearranged everything so you can live the purpose for which He created you!

You have a purpose in this world. And if you're ever unclear about what that purpose is, go to God and ask Him to lay it out. Be reassured when things don't turn out like you thought they would, knowing that whatever happens, all will be well. God is with you, going before you, and protecting you from behind.

Thank You for having a plan, Lord. Show me where You'd have me walk, what You'd have me do!

I know I'm worthy because God re-created me for good works!

GOD REWARDS YOUR PERSEVERANCE

Now He was telling them a parable to show that at all
times they ought to pray and not to lose heart.
LUKE 18:1 NASB

Jesus told the disciples a parable about a judge who didn't fear God or care about people. It seems a widow kept coming to him, telling him her rights were being violated and demanding protection from those against her. But the judge ignored her time and time again. Finally, he said to himself, "Even though I do not fear God nor respect man, yet because this widow bothers me, I will give her legal protection, otherwise by continually coming she will wear me out" (Luke 18:4-5 NASB).

Just as the corrupt judge relented to the widow by stepping into the situation and bringing about justice, our loving God will do right by His faithful who "cry to Him day and night" (Luke 18:7 NASB).

When you are looking for God to right a wrong, to step into your situation, don't stop with one prayer. Continue to cry out to Him, knowing that He, in His compassion, is already working behind the scenes to bring you justice, responding to your pleas. Do not lose heart!

God, here is my plea: In Your compassion, respond
to my prayer. I will not lose heart but will trust You
are setting things right for me—to Your glory!

I know I'm worthy because my compassionate and loving
God hears my prayers and rewards my perseverance!

GOD REWARDS YOUR COMMITMENT TO HIM

*"Remember what happened to Lot's wife! If you grasp
and cling to life on your terms, you'll lose it, but if you
let that life go, you'll get life on God's terms."*
LUKE 17:32–33 MSG

•   •   •   •   •   •   •   •   •   •   •   •   •   •   •

Abraham's cousin Lot was living in the sinful city of Sodom, which God was about to destroy. At Abraham's request, God sent two angels to drag Lot and his family out of town before its destruction. Once the family was safely out of the city, one of the angels told them, "Run for your lives! And don't look back or stop anywhere in the valley!" (Genesis 19:17 NLT). Everyone obeyed—except for Lot's wife. She "looked back as she was following behind him, and she turned into a pillar of salt" (Genesis 19:26 NLT).

Lot's wife was so attached to her material possessions and status in the city that she couldn't help but look back. Because of that, she was destroyed before she could reach safety.

Jesus wants you to learn from Lot's wife. He asks that you not cling to a life lived on your terms but to live your life on God's terms. When you do, you'll gain true life, and He'll reward your commitment to Him!

*Help me, Lord, to be more focused on You than
anything else. I want to live my life on Your terms
because I know that's the best choice I could ever make.*

I know I'm worthy because God rewards me for living for Him!

GOD GIVES YOU DIRECT ACCESS TO HIM

*For it is through Him that we both [whether far off or near]
now have an introduction (access) by one [Holy] Spirit to
the Father [so that we are able to approach Him].*
EPHESIANS 2:18 AMPC

God has always desired that His people be close to Him, come to Him, seek Him, want Him. But then Adam and Eve desired to go their own way, and sin entered the world, separating the holy from the unholy.

Then God sent Jesus. The reconciler. The peacemaker. The one who ended the hostility, eliminated the conflict. The one who has saved those willing to believe. Once again, you can approach the one who calls you His beloved. You have access to the Creator of the world through the Holy Spirit, who presents you before the throne of God. You can come to Him with boldness at any time.

God loved you so much that He allowed His only Son to die on the cross. All so you could come across that gap Jesus has bridged. Draw near to God—and He will be sure to draw near to you (see James 4:8).

I thank You, God, with all my heart for all You have done, all You have allowed to be sacrificed just so I could be close to You once more.

I know I'm worthy because God gives me direct access to Him!

GOD REJOICES OVER YOU

The Lord your God is in the midst of you, a Mighty One, a Savior
[Who saves]! He will rejoice over you with joy; He will rest [in silent
satisfaction] and in His love He will be silent and make no mention
[of past sins, or even recall them]; He will exult over you with singing.
ZEPHANIAH 3:17 AMPC

When you seek God with all your being and follow His ways, He's delighted! As you rejoice in Him and trust Him, He's so happy He sings over you! Because Jesus died for your sins, God makes no mention of your missteps and mistakes. As a believer, your sins have been removed from you "as far as the east is from the west" (Psalm 103:12 NASB).

And God doesn't just sing over you but has planted a new song in your mouth—a hymn of praise to Him. For He's heard your cry, rescued you from destruction, and set you firmly on the ground (see Psalm 40:1–3).

Today consider what God has done for you. Plant in your mind a picture of Him rejoicing over you, pouring out His love, singing over you. Then sing your song of praise—the one He's planted in your heart—to Him. Revel and rejoice together as one!

Lord, You've done so much for me! I'm overwhelmed by Your song.
May I praise You with the new song You've planted within me!

I know I'm worthy because God rejoices over me!

GOD CALLS INTO BEING THINGS THAT WERE NOT

He is our father in the sight of God, in whom he believed—the God who gives life to the dead and calls into being things that were not. Against all hope, Abraham in hope believed and so became the father of many nations, just as it had been said to him, "So shall your offspring be."
ROMANS 4:17–18 NIV

God can do anything in your life. He makes the impossible possible. Just by speaking words, God calls nonexistent things into being!

Imagine being Abraham. God told him he'd be the father of many nations. Yet year after year went by without a son in sight. But Abraham knew his God. He knew God could do the impossible, so he hoped against all hope that he would be given a son, which finally happened when Abraham was one hundred years old and his wife, Sarah, ninety! Why did Abraham believe? Because God had said so! And He alone had the power to work this miracle!

God can do anything at any time, anywhere. Believe in that power, that your loving God can call anything into being. Never lose hope. God *will* come through for you. There is no limit to what He can do to fulfill His desire and meet yours.

God, I know there's no limit to what You can do.
You alone can work miracles in my life!

I know I'm worthy because God calls into being
for His beloved things that never existed!

GOD KEEPS HIS PROMISES

*No unbelief or distrust made him waver (doubtingly question)
concerning the promise of God, but he grew strong and was
empowered by faith as he gave praise and glory to God,
fully satisfied and assured that God was able and mighty
to keep His word and to do what He had promised.*
ROMANS 4:20-21 AMPC

Can you imagine trusting so much in God's promises that, as the years of waiting go by, you grow stronger and more empowered by your faith? Can you imagine praising God for a promise not yet delivered?

That's what Abraham did! And there's more! Because of his amazing trust in God, "his faith was credited to him as righteousness (right standing *with* God)" (Romans 4:22 AMPC, emphasis added). These words and this story were not just recorded for Abraham's benefit, but for yours! God credits *you* as standing right with Him because you believe in Him, the one who brought Jesus to life amid another seemingly hopeless situation (see Romans 4:23-24)!

What promise are you counting on God fulfilling? Follow Abraham's example, and praise God for already bringing it to pass—even if you're still waiting. As you do, you will grow strong, and your faith will empower you!

*God, I'm waiting on this promise. . . .
And I praise You for bringing it to pass!*

I know I'm worthy because God has kept His promise to me!

GOD GIVES YOU REST

*Come to Me, all you who labor and are heavy-laden
and overburdened, and I will cause you to rest.
[I will ease and relieve and refresh your souls.]*
MATTHEW 11:28 AMPC

Author and minister George MacDonald wrote, "Few delights can equal the mere presence of one whom we trust utterly." This is so true! You can relax, be yourself, be calm, and be renewed when you're with someone you know has the best in mind for you. Who will do anything for you. Who loves you just as you love him or her.

Jesus is that person. You can trust Him with your heart, soul, spirit, troubles, and your very life, for He is the one who gave up His lifeblood for you so you could be reconciled to God, the one who will never leave or forsake you. When you are in Jesus' presence, the one who calls you friend, you can tell Him everything that's going on—your problems, your hopes, your dreams. Or you can sit in companionable silence, just soaking in His love.

Today, take time to be with Jesus. Unburden yourself, knowing He can carry your load. You will find all the rest and refreshment you need to continue on the road with Him.

---

*Beloved Jesus, I come to You today knowing
You're waiting to relieve and refresh me.*

I know I'm worthy because God gives me rest!

GOD IS MOVED BY YOUR PRAYERS

After that God was moved by prayer.
2 SAMUEL 21:14 NASB

Someone once said that faith may move mountains, but prayer moves God. That's an amazing statement to ponder, one that may revive your prayer life: to know and understand that what you say to God when you pray from the heart will move God into action on your behalf. What power your prayers yield!

And Jesus has taught you how to pray. He said, "When you pray, go into your [most] private room, and, closing the door, pray to your Father, Who is in secret; and your Father, Who sees in secret, will reward you *in the open*" (Matthew 6:6 AMPC). But how do you know God has heard you? The Bible says that you can be confident that when you ask anything according to His will, God hears you. And because you know He hears you, you know you'll receive what you have asked (see 1 John 5:14–15).

God is moved by your prayers. Plant that knowledge, that fact, that truth deep within your inner being. And your mustard-seed faith will grow beyond what you could ever hope or imagine.

My beloved Father God, I come to You in secret, to have a heart-to-heart talk with You, knowing You hear me and will answer.

I know I'm worthy because God is moved by my prayers!

GOD DELIGHTS IN MY HUMBLE FAITH

For the LORD takes delight in his people;
he crowns the humble with victory.
PSALM 149:4 NIV

Nothing is impossible with God. Those words echo throughout the Bible (see Genesis 18:14; Isaiah 46:10; Matthew 17:20; Matthew 19:26; Mark 9:23; Mark 10:27; Luke 1:37; Luke 18:27; Philippians 4:13). And a myriad of stories proves that truth—God parts the Red Sea, Jesus turns water into wine, the Spirit lifts Philip out of the water, angels break Peter's chains. All it takes is the combination of your humble faith and God's amazing power!

Jeremiah prayed, "Lord God! Behold, You have made the heavens and the earth by Your great power and by Your outstretched arm! There is nothing too hard or too wonderful for You" (Jeremiah 32:17 AMPC). He goes on to say God has His eyes open to people's ways and rewards them accordingly (see Jeremiah 32:19).

When you have a problem and see no solution, when you're trapped in a situation and see no way out, cry out to God with all your heart. Be humble, telling Him, "Lord, we both know I can't do this—but I believe You can!" And He'll meet you in the midst of it all, rewarding you with peace and victory!

Lord, You know what I'm up against. You know I
can't do this—but You can! So I'm leaving this in
Your hands because nothing is too hard for You.

I know I'm worthy because God delights in my humble faith!

GOD WANTS YOUR ALL

*Jesus said to him, "No one, after putting his hand to
the plow and looking back, is fit for the kingdom of God."*
LUKE 9:62 NASB

When Jesus invited people to follow Him, some went immediately, leaving their boats and fishing nets behind. Others refused to follow at all. Then there were the in-betweeners, the ones who asked Jesus questions and, not liking the answers, turned away from Him. Or those who gave excuses as to why they could not continue on with Him, like having to bury a dead family member or wanting to say goodbye to loved ones.

To be fit for the kingdom of God, you need to be totally committed, not looking back. Like a farmer, if your hand is on the plow but your eyes are focused on what's behind you, you'll quickly veer off course and create crooked furrows.

The apostle Paul aspired to "forgetting what lies behind and straining forward to what lies ahead" (Philippians 3:13 AMPC). He pressed "on toward the goal to win the prize for which God has called me heavenward in Christ Jesus" (Philippians 3:14 NIV).

God wants your all—for His sake and your own. So keep looking forward, and you'll see the clear path to God's kingdom!

*Lord, help me be swayed into looking not back to
the world but forward to the prospect of heaven!*

I know I'm worthy because God wants my all
so I can join Him in His kingdom!

GOD SHOWERS YOU WITH BLESSINGS

[My people] shall dwell safely. . .and sleep [confidently]. . . .
And I will make them and the places round about My hill a blessing,
and I will cause the showers to come down in their season; there
shall be showers of blessing [of good insured by God's favor].
EZEKIEL 34:25–26 AMPC

Because you are a believer in Jesus, there is peace between you and God. You have been given His Holy Spirit. Jesus dwells within you, and you now dwell in God. Because of this, you can walk without fear. You can live safely and sleep peacefully. You are filled with hope, courage, strength, and power to do what He's called you to do. And best of all, you can wait for the never-ending showers of blessings that God rains down on you. As George MacDonald, Scottish author, poet, and Christian minister, writes, you will be constantly "waiting for the endless good which He is always giving as fast as He can get us able to take it in."

Look around you today. Take note of all the blessings surrounding you. Dig into the Word, and ask God to reveal the good message He has for you in this quiet moment. Thank God for all He has given you. Expect and look for more blessings to come.

You are so good to me, Lord. Thank You so
much for all You have blessed me with.

I know I'm worthy because God showers me with His blessings!

GOD TRANSFORMS YOUR PANIC TO PRAISE AND PEACE

O God, have mercy on me, for people are hounding me.
My foes attack me all day long.... But when I am afraid,
I will put my trust in you. I praise God for what he has
promised. I trust in God, so why should I be afraid?

PSALM 56:1, 3–4 NLT

Many things can induce panic: threats of war, shootings, terrorist attacks, hurricanes, tornadoes, earthquakes, job loss, health challenges, and so on. As a believer, you can choose a path away from panic. You can rely on your confidence in your mighty God. You can choose to trust Him, knowing He's made certain promises to you. You can remember that, with God on your side, there's nothing any human or circumstances can do to you.

When you place your confidence in God, you're making a conscious decision to respond spiritually instead of reacting emotionally. To get from panic to praise and peace, tell God what's disturbing you. Tell Him you trust Him, that you know that He's in your corner. Recall what God has done in the past, and then praise Him for keeping His promises, affirming His vow to guard you. And soon peace will reign within.

Lord, here's what is happening.... I trust You to see
me through and praise You for what You've promised.
Thank You for the peace that gives me.

I know I'm worthy because God turns my panic to praise and peace!

GOD COLLECTS YOUR TEARS

*You keep track of all my sorrows. You have collected all
my tears in your bottle. You have recorded each one
in your book. . . . This I know: God is on my side!*
PSALM 56:8-9 NLT

Although God may not literally have a bottle containing your tears or a big book of wrongs against you, God does know what you've suffered (see Exodus 3:7). He's not only aware of your entire backstory—as a good friend would be—but He knows all the times you've had a good cry. In fact, He cries with you (see John 11:33-35)!

It's comforting to know that God cares so deeply about you that He weeps when you weep. That He's eager and willing to heal and mend your broken heart, to bind up your wounds (see Psalm 147:3).

So when the blues come calling, cry on God's shoulder. Take heart that He knows what's happening and is on your side. And all the while, take comfort as you remember that one day your loving God "will wipe every tear" from your eyes, "and there will be no more death or sorrow or crying or pain" (Revelation 21:4 NLT).

---

*Thank You, Lord, for loving me so much that You collect my tears!
Mend my broken heart, and reassure me with Your warm embrace
of peace and hope. I rise with courage, knowing You're on my side!*

I know I'm worthy because God collects my tears and gives me courage.

GOD HAS CHOSEN YOU, HOLY AND BELOVED

So, as those who have been chosen of God, holy and beloved,
put on a heart of compassion, kindness, humility, gentleness and
patience; bearing with one another, and forgiving each other. . .
just as the Lord forgave you. . . . Beyond all these things put on love.
COLOSSIANS 3:12–14 NASB

Through His grace, God has chosen you to be His daughter. Because of Jesus' sacrifice and your acceptance of Him in your life, you are now accepted and holy in God's eyes. But when you began to believe, you did not automatically take on the Christlike attributes of compassion, kindness, humility, gentleness, and patience. Yet you now have the responsibility to adopt them.

At the same time, you are to forgive others just as God forgave you. And above all, put on love.

This may sound like a tall order. It's certainly one you cannot fulfill on your own. But there is no need to despair. Simply surrender yourself to the control of God's Spirit. He alone will bring you to the place God wants you to be to become the woman God created you to be—to His glory and your joy!

Lord, I surrender myself to the control of Your Spirit. Help me to
be compassionate, kind, humble, gentle, patient, and forgiving.
Above all, help me give others the love You've given me!

I know I'm worthy because God has chosen me to be like Christ!

GOD PROTECTS AND PROSPERS YOU

Don't worry about the wicked or envy those who do wrong. For like grass, they soon fade away. Like spring flowers, they soon wither. Trust in the LORD and do good. Then you will live safely in the land and prosper.
PSALM 37:1-3 NLT

· · · · · · · · · · · · · · · · ·

It can be difficult to stand by and watch ungodly people gain power, success, and wealth. You may also find it difficult not to envy what the "haves" have. It just doesn't seem fair that those who snub God continue to rise and those who follow Him seemingly fall by the wayside.

Yet even though it *looks* like the ungodly "have it all," God's Word says those who don't stand right with Him will be like grass and flowers, fading away and withering. Meanwhile, because you trust in the Lord and do good things, God promises you'll live safely and prosper!

Consider the demise of the cruel queen Jezebel, who seemed to have it all. After she fixed her hair and makeup, her eunuchs pushed her out a window. She was then trampled by horses and eaten by dogs. All that was left when they came to bury her was her skull, her feet, and the palms of her hands.

So don't worry about the "haves." Instead, trust God. He'll give you the true life!

I'm so glad I long for and trust in You more than wealth or power, Lord. With You I know I'll find true safety and prosperity.

I know I'm worthy because God protects and prospers me!

GOD GIVES YOU YOUR HEART'S DESIRE

Delight yourself also in the Lord, and He will give you the desires and secret petitions of your heart. Commit your way to the Lord [roll and repose each care of your load on Him]; trust (lean on, rely on, and be confident) also in Him and He will bring it to pass.

PSALM 37:4–5 AMPC

The more you keep company with God, the more you'll learn to know Him and His will for your life. And the more you begin to trust and follow Him, the more you'll hear His voice guiding you and see His light revealing the path you should take.

So take steps to delight yourself in the Lord. Spend time reading His Word, sitting with Him, handing Him all your troubles and challenges, and committing your feet to His path. As you do so, your heart's desires will begin to line up with His. That's when God will make your wishes become reality! Those heart's desires will not be the things you want to accomplish apart from God but will be those things that bring you true peace and satisfaction (see Psalm 37:37).

Lord, I find such delight in You and Your ways! Reveal my true heart's desire as I commit all that I am to You. I trust You will bring it to pass!

I know I'm worthy because God grants me my heart's secret desire!

GOD TURNS YOUR MOURNING INTO JOY

*Weeping may stay for the night, but rejoicing comes in the morning.
. . . You turned my wailing into dancing; you removed my sackcloth
and clothed me with joy, that my heart may sing your praises
and not be silent. LORD my God, I will praise you forever.*
PSALM 30:5, 11–12 NIV

David had seen trouble. He had enemies after him, his health was threatened, his soul was in a dark place, and at some point God seemed angry then distant (see Psalm 30:1–3, 5, 7). But in all those instances, David had cried out to God and was lifted above enemies, healed, brought into the light, again favored and helped by God. His wailing was turned into dancing. His mourning suit was taken off and replaced with clothes of joy. At the end, David's heart couldn't help but sing God's praises.

When you're mourning a loss—whether it be that of a loved one, home, marriage, job, or some treasure—don't despair. Although you may do some weeping, have confidence that God will turn your mourning into joy. God promises to make all things work together for good (see Romans 8:28).

*Thank You, Lord, for always being there when I need You,
for helping me to understand this mourning will one
day pass, and for turning my darkness into light!*

I know I'm worthy because God transforms my sorrow to joy!

GOD GIFTS YOU WITH LOVE, GRACE, AND FAITH

It is by grace you have been saved, through faith—and this is not from yourselves, it is the gift of God—not by works, so that no one can boast.
Ephesians 2:8-9 niv

The only reason God sent His Son Jesus into the world is because He loves you and wants to save you. The apostle John makes this clear when he writes, "God showed how much he loved us by sending his one and only Son into the world so that we might have eternal life through him. This is real love—not that we loved God, but that he loved us and sent his Son as a sacrifice to take away our sins" (1 John 4:9-10 NLT). When you accepted Jesus, God forgave you, granted you life everlasting, and gave you the Holy Spirit to help you find the way.

That means there is nothing you can ever do—no good works, money, or any other effort—to earn the gifts of saving grace and faith. It's a done deal! Revel in that knowledge today!

*I am amazed, Lord, at what You have so freely given to me—
and all because You love me! I am so filled with joy from
that knowledge. Thank You, Father, for your precious gifts
of love, faith, and grace, which I can never repay.*

I know I'm worthy because God has given
me the gifts of love, grace, and faith!

GOD LEADS YOU BY THE HAND

Your path led through the sea, your way through the mighty waters, though your footprints were not seen. You led your people like a flock by the hand of Moses and Aaron.
PSALM 77:19-20 NIV

Can you imagine being one of the Israelites who had to walk on the sands of the parted Red Sea, huge walls of water on each side? What courage it must have taken for them and their families to make that crossing.

Many Old Testament stories of endurance, challenges, and dangers were taken down so that God's people might learn from them and take from them encouragement and hope (see Romans 15:4). From the story of the Red Sea crossing (see Exodus 14) and today's verses from the psalms, it's clear that at times God may lead you through places that seem a little scary and down pathways you would never have thought open. Like the Israelites, although you may not see God's footprints on the path before you, you can be sure God is leading you through the mighty waters, that His presence is very real.

Wherever God leads, be assured you are safe with Him and that He'll never let go of your hand.

Although I cannot see Your face or footprints, I know You are with me. Lead me where You would have me go, and I will walk willingly. My trust is in You.

I know I'm worthy because God leads me by my hand!

GOD WILL NEVER FAIL TO LOVE YOU

You are a God of forgiveness, gracious and merciful, slow to become angry, and rich in unfailing love. You did not abandon them.
NEHEMIAH 9:17 NLT

After the exiled Israelites rebuilt the Jerusalem wall, the priests led all the people in a prayer that begins by praising God. It then retells their history, from creation to Abraham, to the wandering in the wilderness, to the Israelites' exile and return (see Nehemiah 9).

Throughout the prayer, God's miracles are described, as are all the times God's people rebelled against Him. Yet the recounting makes clear that no matter what God's children did or how often they strayed, God never abandoned them. As a pillar of cloud by day and of fire by night, He continued to lead them. He continued to send His Spirit to instruct them. He never stopped supplying heaven-sent manna for their hunger and water for their thirst (see Nehemiah 9:19-20).

Your God has so much love for you that no matter how many times you stray or rebel, He will continue to forgive, to be gracious to you and show you mercy. His anger will be slow and temporary, and He'll always love you. That's how much you matter to Him.

Lord, I thank You for being so patient with me and loving me no matter what. May I be as gracious, patient, and loving toward others.

I know I'm worthy because my God never stops loving me!

GOD MANIFESTS HIS POWERS AMID YOUR WEAKNESS

My grace (My favor and loving-kindness and mercy) is enough for you [sufficient against any danger and enables you to bear the trouble manfully]; for My strength and power are made perfect (fulfilled and completed) and show themselves most effective in [your] weakness.

2 CORINTHIANS 12:9 AMPC

The apostle Paul had a thorn in his side, some infirmity that he wrestled with, so he pleaded for the Lord to rid him of it. That's when Christ told Paul that His grace, love, kindness, and mercy were all Paul needed to bear through whatever assailed him. In fact, Christ's power showed itself even more effective in Paul's weakness!

That response from Christ prompted Paul to write, "Therefore, I will all the more gladly glory in my weaknesses *and* infirmities, that the strength *and* power of Christ (the Messiah) may rest (yes, may pitch a tent over and dwell) upon me!" (2 Corinthians 12:9 AMPC).

Imagine that the glory of God, as well as the awesome strength and amazing power of His Son, actually pitches its tent upon you when you are at your weakest! Revel and take strength in that knowledge today!

I'm so amazed that I can endure anything and everything when I have Your love, Lord! May Your tent rest over me as a demonstration of Your power!

I know I'm worthy because God chooses to pitch His tent of love and strength over me!

GOD RESTS YOUR SOUL

*Thus says the LORD, "Stand by the ways and see
and ask for the ancient paths, where the good way is,
and walk in it; and you will find rest for your souls."*
JEREMIAH 6:16 NASB

Psalm 116 begins with the writer stating how much he loves God because God hears his cry. He talks about the distress and anguish he'd suffered and how he asked God to save him. After God does so, he sings to himself, "Return to your rest, O my soul, for the LORD has dealt bountifully with you" (Psalm 116:7 NASB).

Jesus also speaks about your soul, saying, "Take My yoke upon you and learn from Me, for I am gentle and humble in heart, and YOU WILL FIND REST FOR YOUR SOULS" (Matthew 11:29 NASB). The latter part of this verse is a direct quote from Jeremiah 6:16 above.

God's message is clear. In Him alone does your soul find true rest. On His path alone, His good way, your soul finds the relief, refreshment, quiet, and rest that it craves. Ask God to show you His path. Walk it, and your soul will find its ease, no matter what comes your way.

---

*I'm calling upon You today, Lord, to show me the good
way You would have me go. There my soul will find
the blessed quiet, the peace, and the rest it craves.*

I know I'm worthy because my God provides the rest my soul craves.

GOD TRANSFORMS YOUR MIND

*Don't copy the behavior and customs of this world, but let
God transform you into a new person by changing the
way you think. Then you will learn to know God's will
for you, which is good and pleasing and perfect.*
ROMANS 12:2 NLT

Sometimes it may seem hard not to follow the fleeting fashions of the world, but God wants a better path for you. He wants you to allow Him to mold you into the person He created you to be, to change the way you think, to open your mind so that He can point you toward what He wills for you.

Your path to God's transformation of you begins with His Word, spending time in it, meditating on it. Doing so will renew your thoughts. It will also change your heart as you begin to know Him better, depend on and trust in Him more.

Your thoughts will be God-inspired, and you'll find your way as you follow their leading. You will find yourself moving at His impulses, not your own. And His way will become your way—good, pleasing, and perfect.

*Show me Your way, Lord. Transform my mind, change
my heart, so that I find Your will and way for my feet—
a good, pleasing, and perfect path to follow.*

I know I'm worthy because my God transforms
my mind so that I can find His way.

GOD SURROUNDS YOU WITH HIS POWER

"Don't be afraid!" Elisha told him. "For there are more on our side than on theirs!" Then Elisha prayed, "O LORD, open his eyes and let him see!" The LORD opened the young man's eyes, and when he looked up, he saw that the hillside around Elisha was filled with horses and chariots of fire.

2 KINGS 6:16–17 NLT

The king of Aram kept planning ambushes against Israel. But his plans were continually thwarted by the prophet Elisha, who would tell Israel's king where the ambushes were being set. Angered, the king of Aram decided to seize Elisha, who resided in the city of Dothan.

One day Elisha's servant awoke, went out, and was alarmed by seeing the enemy army had surrounded the city with horses and chariots. Panicked, he asked Elisha, "What will we do now?" (2 Kings 6:15 NLT). Elisha told him not to be afraid because they had a greater army on their side. Then he prayed that God would open his servant's eyes. When He did, the man saw God's horses and chariots of fire.

You need never fear any "army" that comes against you, because God has you surrounded by His heavenly power. Just open your spiritual eyes, and you'll see it!

Lord, I know I don't need to fear anything, because Your heavenly power is all around me, shielding me from harm! Thank You for Your heavenly protection!

I know I'm worthy because my God surrounds me with His power!

GOD WALKS WITH YOU AMID THE FIRE

*"Look! I see four men walking around in the fire, unbound
and unharmed, and the fourth looks like a son of the gods."*
DANIEL 3:25 NIV

King Nebuchadnezzar of Babylon sent for three men of Israel—Shadrach, Meshach, and Abednego—who reportedly would not worship a golden image he'd made. When he threatened to throw them into a furnace as punishment, they said, "If we are thrown into the blazing furnace, the God we serve is able to deliver us from it, and he will deliver us. . . . But even if he does not . . .we will not serve your gods or worship the image of gold you have set up" (Daniel 3:17-18 NIV). So the king had them tied up and thrown into the flames!

When the king looked into the furnace, he saw a fourth person walking around in the fire with them, one who looked like a son of the gods! After calling the three men out, he saw they were unharmed and unbound, their clothes were intact, and not even the smell of smoke was on them! Because of their faith, Nebuchadnezzar praised God and promoted the men!

Know that God is with you—even when you walk through fire. When you stand with God, God stands with you.

---

*Remind me all my days, Lord, of how You
stand with me when I stand up for You!*

I know I'm worthy because my God walks with me through fire!

GOD'S WORD POINTS YOU TO SUCCESS

They went out and got into the boat, but that night they caught nothing. . . . He [Jesus] said, "Throw your net on the right side of the boat and you will find some." When they did, they were unable to haul the net in because of the large number of fish.

JOHN 21:3, 6 NIV

After the resurrected Jesus had appeared to the disciples in the upper room, Simon Peter decided to go fishing. So several other disciples joined him in the boat. All night, they caught nothing. When dawn was breaking, Jesus was on the beach, although the men did not yet realize it was Him.

Jesus yelled out, asking if they'd caught any fish. When they said no, He told them to throw their net on the right side of the boat. When they did, they caught 153 large fish—yet their net never broke under the weight of their bounty!

Just as Jesus continued to care and provide for His followers, He continues to care and provide for you when you trust and obey His directions. His Word will always point you to the bounty that awaits. Simply follow His lead.

*Lord, You always know and provide just what I need.
Help me stay alert to Your Word and obedient to
Your direction. Point me to the bounty that awaits.*

I know I'm worthy because God uses His Word to point me to success!

GOD CALLS YOU PRECIOUS

I have called you by your name; you are Mine. When you pass through the waters, I will be with you, and through the rivers, they will not overwhelm you. When you walk through the fire, you will not be burned or scorched, nor will the flame kindle upon you. For I am the Lord your God.

ISAIAH 43:1–3 AMPC

God has called you—by your very own name. He knows exactly who you are and has claimed you for Himself. Through Isaiah, God tells you, "You are precious in My sight and honored, and because I love you" (Isaiah 43:4 AMPC).

And it's because of God's great love for you that He promises to walk with you through any situation, challenge, trial, temptation, or ordeal you may find yourself in. He'll be with you through flooding waters and rapid rivers, keeping your head above the water. If you find yourself walking amid flames, He will be with you as He was with Shadrach, Meshach, and Abednego (see Daniel 3). He is your loving God, and you are His precious daughter.

So do not fear or doubt. Have courage and faith, knowing God is with you through this life and beyond.

I feel so valued in Your eyes, Lord, for to You I am precious. I put my hand in Yours, Father God. Let's walk!

I know I'm worthy because God has called me by name!

GOD BLESSES AND MULTIPLIES YOUR OFFERING

Jesus took the five loaves and two fish, looked up toward heaven, and blessed them. . . . Afterward, the disciples picked up twelve baskets of leftover bread and fish. A total of 5,000 men and their families were fed.

MARK 6:41, 43–44 NLT

•   •   •   •   •   •   •   •   •   •   •   •   •   •   •

Jesus had just finished preaching to and teaching a large crowd of people. When the day grew late, the disciples proposed that Jesus send the people away so they could find some food to eat in the nearby villages. But Jesus said, "You feed them" (Mark 6:37 NLT). The disciples told Him they had nothing to feed them with and not enough money to buy all the food the crowd would require. So Jesus sent them off to see what food they could find among the people. The men returned with five loaves of bread and two fish.

Jesus took their meager offering, looked toward heaven, blessed it, and kept giving the disciples food to hand out. At the end, all were fed and much was left over.

When you bring to Jesus whatever you have—talents, money, resources, intangibles, and so on—and offer it to Him, be assured that He will bless it and multiply it for your benefit, the good of others, and His glory. It's a win-win-win!

Lord, here's what I have to offer. Please bless it for Your glory!

I know I'm worthy because God blesses and multiplies my offering!

GOD'S GIVEN WORD NEVER FAILS

*With God nothing is ever impossible and no word from
God shall be without power or impossible of fulfillment.*
LUKE 1:37 AMPC

When the angel Gabriel visited Mary, he had some astonishing news. She
was to become the mother of the Son of God. When she, a virgin, asked how
this would happen, the angel explained, "The Holy Spirit will come upon you,
and the power of the Most High will overshadow you" (Luke 1:35 AMPC). And
from this encounter a holy child would result. Gabriel then told Mary her
once-barren and aged cousin Elizabeth had also conceived and was already
six months along! He ended these revelations by saying that nothing was
impossible with God and no word of His ever failed.

To all this, Mary responded with, "Behold, I am the handmaiden of the
Lord; let it be done to me according to what you have said" (Luke 1:38 AMPC).

Every ordinary girl can live an extraordinary life when she trusts in God,
obeys His will, believes nothing is impossible with God, and is assured His
words are full of power and will be fulfilled.

Believe these truths, and live the extraordinary life God has planned for you!

*With You, Lord, nothing is impossible! Your powerful word
never fails! On these truths I base my faith and my life.*

I know I'm worthy because God has given me His word—
which never fails and makes the impossible possible!

GOD IS YOUR PROTECTIVE WALL OF FIRE

"'And I myself will be a wall of fire around it,'
declares the Lord, 'and I will be its glory within.'"
ZECHARIAH 2:5 NIV

Speaking through Zechariah, God tells His people that He will be a wall of fire around Jerusalem and her glory within. Just as Jerusalem was God's, so you, as a believer, are His. God wants Himself and His words to be the wall of fire that surrounds you, protecting you. God was the pillar of fire guiding the Israelites; He and His Word are the pillar of fire that leads you through the wilderness of life.

God and His Word are also the fire burning within you. When, after His resurrection, the at-first-unrecognized Jesus left the two men traveling to Emmaus, they remarked to each other, "Were not our hearts greatly moved *and* burning within us while He was talking with us on the road and as He opened *and* explained to us [the sense of] the Scriptures?" (Luke 24:32 AMPC). And in Jeremiah 23:29 (NLT), God said, "Does not my word burn like fire?"

Imagine God's protective fire surrounding you and His Word burning within you. Allow God to set your life ablaze in this good way as you realize these blessings in your midst.

Lord, be my wall of fire without and the glory burning within!

I know I'm worthy because God and His Word are
the wall of fire around me and the flame within.

GOD FAVORS TENDER HEARTS

Never before had there been a king like Josiah, who turned to the LORD with all his heart and soul and strength, obeying all the laws of Moses. And there has never been a king like him since.
2 KINGS 23:25 NLT

Josiah began reigning as king of Judah when he was eight years old. Unlike many kings before him who followed foreign gods, he followed the one true God. When the book of law was found in the temple and read to Josiah, he tore his clothes in despair. He sent his priests to discover the consequences of the people not having obeyed God's law. They found a prophetess named Huldah who sent word to Josiah, "Because your heart was [tender and] penitent and you humbled yourself before the Lord when you heard what I said against this place. . .your eyes shall not see all the evil which I will bring on this place" (2 Kings 22:19–20 AMPC).

Throughout Josiah's life, God favored the boy who became a king like no other.

Turn to God with a loving and tender heart, and you'll find yourself greatly favored by God as you serve and obey Him with all your heart, strength, and soul.

My tender heart is open to You, Lord. Speak, and I will humbly serve and obey You with all my heart, strength, and soul.

I know I'm worthy because God favors my tender heart.

GOD BROUGHT YOU TO THIS PLACE AND TIME

If you keep silent at this time, relief and deliverance shall arise for the Jews from elsewhere, but you and your father's house will perish. And who knows but that you have come to the kingdom for such a time as this and for this very occasion?
ESTHER 4:14 AMPC

Esther was an orphaned Jewish girl who lived in Persia and had been raised by her cousin Mordecai. When King Ahasuerus became dissatisfied and angered by his queen, he began looking for another. Esther, who had kept her Jewish identity secret, was chosen to become a part of Ahasuerus' harem and eventually his new queen!

Sometime later, the king's evil official, named Haman, devised a plan to have all the Jews killed. That's when Mordecai sent word to Esther. She was their last hope to thwart Haman's plans and save her people. He said, "Who knows but that you have come to the kingdom for such a time as this?"

Just as God had a plan for Esther's life, He has a plan for yours. God has brought you to this particular place and time to live your life purpose. Trust Him, and He'll help you find your way to bless His people.

Show me, Lord, what You have brought me here to do.
I trust You to help me find Your path and purpose for me.

I know I'm worthy because God has brought me to this time and place—for His people.

GOD SURROUNDS YOU WITH HIS SHIELD OF LOVE

Let all who take refuge in you rejoice; let them sing joyful praises forever. Spread your protection over them, that all who love your name may be filled with joy. For you bless the godly, O LORD; you surround them with your shield of love.
PSALM 5:11–12 NLT

When trouble assails you, to whom do you run? If your answer is to God, you're in a good place. When you run to Him for refuge, you'll find yourself reveling in joy. That's because He knows you trust Him to take care of you, to cover you with His Spirit and protect you. Assured of your love, He wants to shower you with His own in return.

Yet God won't just shower you with His love, He'll *shield* you with it. And because God Himself is the personification of love, it means that *He* is the one surrounding you, protecting you from head to toe.

There are so many benefits to trusting, running to, and relying on the God who created the entire universe and beyond. That's a lot of love, protection, and shielding. That's a lot of God! And He's doing it just for you!

Lord, I'm overwhelmed by the vastness of You and Your love. I'm running to You now. Surround me with Your shield of love as I trust in and cherish You!

I know I'm worthy because God surrounds me with His shield of love.

GOD CONTINUALLY RESCUES YOU

Daniel was brought and cast into the den of lions.
The king said to Daniel, May your God, Whom you
are serving continually, deliver you!
DANIEL 6:16 AMPC

Daniel had been deported from Judah and taken to Babylon, where he worked for three kings. The last, King Darius, was so impressed with Daniel's wisdom, trustworthiness, and ability that he put him in charge of the entire kingdom!

Those officials jealous of Daniel plotted to usurp him. So they coerced Darius into signing a law saying that those who prayed to anyone other than the king would be thrown into the lions' den. Soon Daniel, who diligently prayed three times a day to God, found himself in the lions' den, much to the king's dismay. Yet Daniel survived because God "sent His angel and has shut the lions' mouths" (Daniel 6:22 AMPC).

God rescues all those who serve, trust, and are faithful to Him, because, like you, they are the apples of His eye.

Thank You, Lord, for continuing to rescue me as I stay faithful to You.
I trust in You alone to deliver me today, tomorrow, and forever!

I know I'm worthy because God continually rescues me.

GOD EQUIPS YOU

"You come to me with sword, spear, and javelin, but I come to you in the name of the LORD of Heaven's Armies. . . ." So David triumphed over the Philistine with only a sling and a stone, for he had no sword.
1 SAMUEL 17:45, 50 NLT

When the shepherd boy David finally convinced King Saul that the God who rescued him from lions and bears would rescue him from the giant Goliath, the king gave David his own battle gear to wear: "a bronze helmet and a coat of mail" (1 Samuel 17:38 NLT). But after strapping the sword over the borrowed armor, David realized he could barely walk. So he took it off and "picked up five smooth stones from a stream and put them into his shepherd's bag. Then, armed only with his shepherd's staff and sling, he started across the valley to fight the Philistine" (1 Samuel 17:40 NLT). In the end, it was God's power, David's sling and faith, and one stone that brought down the giant Goliath.

When challenged by the giants in your life, trust that God has already equipped you with everything you need to triumph. For He, working through you, is your greatest weapon!

I'm blessed to have You clothe and equip me in Your power, Lord. As I trust in You, I'm ready to face any challenge that comes before me—in Your name!

I know I'm worthy because God equips me with everything I need to triumph.

GOD ESPECIALLY BLESSES YOU—FOR YOU'VE NOT SEEN YET STILL BELIEVE!

*Then Jesus told him, "You believe because you have seen
me. Blessed are those who believe without seeing me."*
JOHN 20:29 NLT

The first person the resurrected Jesus appeared to was Mary Magdalene. Later that same day, Jesus appeared to the disciples, who were meeting in the upper room behind locked doors for they were afraid of the Jewish leaders. The only disciple who wasn't there that night was Thomas. When the others told him they'd seen Jesus, Thomas said, "I won't believe it unless I see the nail wounds in his hands, put my fingers into them, and place my hand into the wound in his side" (John 20:25 NLT).

Eight days later, Jesus appeared to the disciples again, and Thomas was with them. Jesus told him to put his finger in His wounds and then said, "Don't be faithless any longer. Believe!" (John 20:27 NLT). And Thomas did, prompting Jesus to tell him, "You believe because you have seen me. Blessed are those who believe without seeing me."

You, woman, are one of "those" Jesus has blessed, for you have believed without needing to see the physical evidence. You believe Jesus at His word. Your sown confidence reaps Jesus' blessing—now and forevermore!

---

*I do believe, Jesus! You're my Savior. I believe You at Your word
and see You through Your Word. That seeing is my believing!*

I know I'm worthy because God especially blesses me.

GOD CARRIES YOU IN HIS ARMS

GOD, the Master, comes in power, ready to go into action.
He is going to pay back his enemies and reward those who
have loved him. Like a shepherd, he will care for his flock,
gathering the lambs in his arms, hugging them as he
carries them, leading the nursing ewes to good pasture.
ISAIAH 40:10–11 MSG

God has many facets. The same Lord who comes in power to defend you and annihilate your enemies cares for you like a loving and gentle Shepherd. Because you have faith in Him and love Him, the Shepherd who protects you and shields you from all dangers is longing to reward you.

God reaches out to and picks up the feeblest and weakest in His flock. At times they grow weary trying to keep up with the rest of the sheep. He hugs these lambs to Himself as He carries them along. While He walks, He leads the nursing mothers to a good pasture, where they can find the fuel that will help them take care of the little lambs.

Today, trust that God is carrying you when you are weary and leading you to nourishment when you need strength. This Good Shepherd loves you like no other.

Thank You for lifting me up, Lord, when I'm weary, loving me,
hugging me, protecting me, nourishing me. I yield to Your gentle hand.

I know I'm worthy because God gently carries me in His arms.

GOD NEVER DISAPPOINTS YOU

In my distress I prayed to the LORD, and the LORD answered me
and set me free. The LORD is for me, so I will have no fear....
It is better to take refuge in the LORD than to trust in people.
It is better to take refuge in the LORD than to trust in princes.
PSALM 118:5–6, 8–9 NLT

It may be hard to imagine, but there will be people you trust who will, at some point, disappoint you in some way. It may be a family member who doesn't come through on a promise. A friend who passed your secret on to someone else. A coworker who said something behind your back. A politician who didn't stay true to his or her word. An admired celebrity who was found to be lacking basic morals. A fellow congregant who wasn't there when you needed her.

The psalmist makes clear that it's better to take refuge in and trust in God than in people or princes. "No man who believes in Him [who adheres to, relies on, and trusts in Him] will [ever] be put to shame or be disappointed" (Romans 10:11 AMPC). Trust in God. He'll be there every time, true to His Word.

I feel safe, secure, and loved in You, Lord.
You never let me down. It's in You alone I'll trust.

I know I'm worthy because God never disappoints me.

GOD HELPS YOU, HOLDING YOUR RIGHT HAND

"Don't be afraid, for I am with you. Don't be discouraged, for I am your God. I will strengthen you and help you. I will hold you up with my victorious right hand. . . . For I hold you by your right hand—I, the LORD your God. And I say to you, 'Don't be afraid. I am here to help you. . . . I will help you.' "

ISAIAH 41:10, 13–14 NLT

Through Isaiah, God could not have made it any clearer. He wants you to know you're never to be anxiously looking around. He assures you that you need not be afraid because He—the source, provider, Creator, Redeemer, refuge, and fortress—is right here with you. God commands you to never be discouraged. He will not only help you; He will strengthen you, holding you up with His hand. Anyone and anything battling you will "be as nothing and non-existent" (Isaiah 41:12 NASB).

God has you by your right hand. He's speaking to you, saying, "Don't fear anything. I'm here to help. YOU WILL BE HELPED!"

Picture yourself being lifted in God's right hand while He holds your right. Hear His voice telling you not to fear. See all things coming against you as dust. What a picture of a God who loves you with all His might!

Lord, I hear You! You are all the help and strength I need!

I know I'm worthy because God helps me and holds me by the hand.

GOD GIVES YOU A NEW SONG TO SING

He has given me a new song to sing, a hymn of praise to our God. . . . Oh, the joys of those who trust the LORD. . . . May all who search for you be filled with joy and gladness in you.

PSALM 40:3-4, 16 NLT

The more time you spend getting to know God and recognizing how He's working in your life, the more joyful you become! The more you love, trust, and praise Him!

God has put a new song of praise in your mouth. Why not sing that worship song to Him as soon as your eyes open in the morning? When you do, you'll be sure to begin your day seeing things from God's perspective. You'll be reaffirming how much you're loved, cared for, protected, and looked out for by your mighty Lord. To begin, try singing "I Will Sing of the Mercies of the Lord Forever," a song based on Psalm 89:1. It's an easy one to learn if you don't already know it. Even better, make up one of your own! Either way, the song of praise you sing to God will spark the flame of unsurpassable joy within—and without.

You've given me a song to sing, Lord. May the words from my mouth and the tune from my heart be pleasing to You, the one so deserving of praise.

I know I'm worthy because God has given me a new song to sing.

GOD ENABLES YOU

*"I'm sending you to Pharaoh to bring my people, the People
of Israel, out of Egypt." Moses answered God, "But why me?
What makes you think that I could ever go to Pharaoh and lead
the children of Israel out of Egypt?" "I'll be with you," God said.*
EXODUS 3:10–12 MSG

• • • • • • • • • • • • • • • •

When Moses encountered God speaking out of a burning bush, he learned
what God was calling him to do: bring His people out of Egypt. Moses' first
response was, "Why me? What makes you think this is even something I can
do?" God simply answered, "No worries. I'll be with you."

Moses soon after asked, "Why will anyone think You've sent me?" God
responded by teaching Moses how to use his staff to work God-powered
miracles. Later, Moses asked why he should be sent by God to speak to
Pharaoh, since he (Moses) was slow of speech and tongue. God said Aaron
would be his mouthpiece.

When God gives you a calling, He also enables you to fulfill it by
equipping you with His presence, power, and words. And He provides
all the tools you'll need. With God, you are more than good enough to do
anything, for He is with you.

---

*Thank You, Lord, for making me more than good enough
to do what You are calling me to do. With Your presence,
power, and words, I cannot and will not fail.*

I know I'm worthy because God enables me to fulfill my calling.

GOD MAKES YOUR DAY

This is the day the LORD has made. We will rejoice and be glad in it.
PSALM 118:24 NLT

God makes a new day for you every day. Because of His faithfulness to you, His mercies are new every morning (see Lamentations 3:23–24). With each breaking dawn, you have a new opportunity to see your day as a gift from God, to expect He will be working things out for your good (see Romans 8:28), to reaffirm your trust in Him.

Today, if you keep your heart tender, you will hear God's voice telling you the way you should go (see Hebrews 3:7–8). If you keep your eyes open, you will see God opening doors before you (see Revelation 3:8). If you stay close to God's Word, you will see how much He favors you, the loving daughter He knows by name (see Exodus 33:17). You may even encounter something God has been planning for you all along, something He has prepared that is beyond what you could ever have imagined (see 1 Corinthians 2:9).

Begin your day trusting in the one who makes your day, and you will find yourself rejoicing at everything that comes your way!

I am thrilled to be with You, Lord, on this new day You have made! I will rejoice and be so glad in it!

I know I'm worthy because God makes my day!

GOD COMMANDS HIS ANGELS TO GUARD YOU

If you say, "The LORD is my refuge," and you make the Most High your dwelling, no harm will overtake you, no disaster will come near your tent. For he will command his angels concerning you to guard you in all your ways.
PSALM 91:9–11 NIV

• • • • • • • • • • • • • • • • •

When you put yourself under God's care, relying on Him during difficulties and dangers, trusting He will protect you, and actively communing with Him, no harm can come to you. You will be covered by His holy and supreme presence. But that's not all. When you admit that God is indeed your refuge, He will order His angels to guard you. He bids them to secure your safety, to be a shield to your body, soul, and spirit. When you walk in God's way, God's angels keep you in your way.

Just as angels protected Daniel in the lions' den, warned Joseph (Jesus' foster father) of danger, and were with Jesus for His birth, life, death, and resurrection, God's angels protect, warn, and accompany you (see Hebrews 1:14). They are heaven-sent protection from a God who adores you. Is there any greater love?

Once again, Lord, I find myself speechless. There are so many ways You care for me as I dwell beneath Your wings. Thank You so much for the gift of Your angels.

I know I'm worthy because God commands His angels to protect me!

GOD GIVES YOU TRANQUILITY OF MIND AND SLEEP

*In peace I will both lie down and sleep, for You, Lord,
alone make me dwell in safety and confident trust.*
PSALM 4:8 AMPC

In Psalm 4, King David shares his formula for acquiring a good night's rest. It begins with a prayer to God, asking Him to answer when David calls. He remembers how God has freed him from his troubles in the past. He affirms how the Lord sets apart the godly—people who love, are kind, and trust Him. How God listens when they speak to Him. David reminds himself to meditate in his heart while he lies upon the bed, to be still before God. He asks God to smile upon him and remembers that the joy God gives him is greater than those who've reaped an abundant harvest.

At the end, David is ready to lie down and sleep, telling God (and in the process, himself) that it is He alone who makes him dwell in safety.

God wants you, dear daughter, to have the same peace of mind when you are ready to say good night.

---

*Lord, I want to fall asleep remembering it is You alone
who makes me safe. That You listen when I speak,
hear and answer my prayers, and smile down upon me.
You are my joy as I fall asleep in Your protective arms.*

I know I'm worthy because God gives me tranquility of mind and sleep!

GOD WANTS TO HEAR—
AND GRANT—YOUR DESIRE

"What do you want me to do for you?" Jesus asked.
"My Rabbi," the blind man said, "I want to see!"
MARK 10:51 NLT

As Jesus, His disciples, and a crowd were heading out of Jericho, a blind man named Bartimaeus cried out, asking Jesus to have mercy on him. People tried to keep Bartimaeus quiet, but that only made him shout louder.

When Jesus heard Bartimaeus, He stopped and told the others to tell the man to come to Him. Hearing that Jesus was calling him, Bartimaeus threw off his coat, lest it hinder him from getting to Jesus, and ran to Him.

Jesus wanted to hear what Bartimaeus wished of Him. When his desire was made clear, Jesus told him it was his faith that had healed him. At that moment, the blind man could see.

God wants you to tell Him exactly what you desire. It's not that He doesn't already know. It's that it brings Him joy to hear His beloved's request, and it's good for you to put it into words, having faith it will be granted. He has said, "If you remain in me and my words remain in you, you may ask for anything you want, and it will be granted" (John 15:7 NLT).

Lord, I'm Your beloved. Let me tell You from the heart what I desire.

I know I'm worthy because God wants to hear—and grant—my desire.

GOD GIVES POWER TO THE FAINT WHO WAIT

Those who wait for the Lord [who expect, look for, and hope in Him] shall change and renew their strength and power; they shall lift their wings and mount up [close to God] as eagles [mount up to the sun]; they shall run and not be weary, they shall walk and not faint or become tired.
ISAIAH 40:31 AMPC

God never runs out of strength or energy. Nothing can exhaust Him. He is the all-powerful and mighty God. Yet He knows that His people—young and old—can run themselves down, can burn out, trying to do all they feel they need or wish to do, whether it be in the home, on the job, or serving at church!

When you desperately need energy and strength, when you're about to faint from exhaustion, go to God. He'll give you power and give you abundant strength. Your job is to wait on Him to do so, to look for and expect Him to reenergize you. He'll reward your patience by renewing you. Trust Him to give you the strength to fly like an eagle, mounting up ever closer to God.

I'm so tired, Lord. I'm looking and expecting strength and power from You, in Your time. You alone can renew me—mind, body, spirit, and soul—so I can soar like the eagle, close to You.

I know I'm worthy because God renews my power as I wait for Him.

GOD, THROUGH HIS WORD, PREPARES YOU FOR YOUR TASKS

Every part of Scripture is God-breathed and useful one way or another—showing us truth, exposing our rebellion, correcting our mistakes, training us to live God's way. Through the Word we are put together and shaped up for the tasks God has for us.
2 TIMOTHY 3:16–17 MSG

Like any good father, God has not left you alone to find your way in the dark as you live this life for Him. He has left His Word for you to read, study, and meditate on. This God-breathed text shows you the truth you need to live by so that you can be trained to do what is right in His eyes. His Word shapes you, reforms you, equips you so that you can take on the tasks, the good works, He has assigned to you.

As you trust in God and study His Word, you'll become inspired as you follow His direction and instruction. You'll gain wisdom as you ask the Holy Spirit to help you apply the scriptures to your life.

God's light continues to shine on you from His Word. Allow it to illuminate your life, and you will be prepared for anything God calls you to do.

Holy Spirit, teach me how to apply my Lord's Word to my life. Show me what You would have me know as I open its pages today.

I know I'm worthy because God, through His Word, prepares me for my tasks.

GOD HAS AN UNBREAKABLE HOLD ON YOU

Listen to the LORD who created you. . . . "Do not be afraid, for I have ransomed you. I have called you by name; you are mine. . . . From eternity to eternity I am God. No one can snatch anyone out of my hand. No one can undo what I have done."

ISAIAH 43:1, 13 NLT

Listen up! God commands you to have no fear—of anything. He has saved you in a big way. You're safe in His hands, under His protection. Jesus has paid the ransom for your life, spirit, and soul.

God not only knows your name, He calls you by it. You're now His eternal possession. No one can ever snatch you away from Him. No matter what your circumstances are, He can and will deliver you out of them and bring you safely back to His loving arms. No devil, no evil, no man, no woman, no army, no king can come between you and God and His plans for you.

Trust that nothing and no one can undo what God has already done for you. He will never let you go. In His presence, you're safe and sound. No longer lost. Always found—in Him.

I have no fear because You are near, Lord, and always will be. Amen!

I know I'm worthy because God has an unbreakable hold on me.

GOD TURNS CURSES INTO BLESSINGS FOR YOU

The LORD your God refused to listen to Balaam. He turned the intended curse into a blessing because the LORD your God loves you.
DEUTERONOMY 23:5 NLT

• • • • • • • • • • • • • • •

When Balak, the king of Moab, saw the seemingly undefeatable Israelites camping near him, he was afraid they'd attack him and his people, so he offered lots of riches to a man named Balaam in exchange for his cursing the Israelites. But Balaam told Balak he'd say only what God told him to say. It followed that each of the three times Balak asked Balaam to curse the Israelites, Balaam ended up blessing God's people instead. Each time "God turned the curse into a blessing" (Nehemiah 13:2 NLT). (For the full story, check out Numbers 22–24.)

God says, "No weapon that is formed against you will prosper" (Isaiah 54:17 NASB). Why? Because "the LORD your God loves you."

So the next time something unexpected and unwarranted comes your way, don't panic. Stand strong in God. You can be sure He will turn everything that happens in your life into a blessing. Just wait and see.

Lord, You are so good to me. I am comforted, encouraged, and strengthened in the knowledge that You will turn all things that fill me with dread, alarm, or fear into a blessing! And all because You love me so much. Thank You, Lord.

I know I'm worthy because God turns curses into blessings for me.

GOD WILL NEVER FORGET YOU

"Can a woman forget her nursing child and have no compassion on the son of her womb? Even these may forget, but I will not forget you. Behold, I have inscribed you on the palms of My hands."
ISAIAH 49:15–16 NASB

Nursing mothers are very attentive and attuned to their babies. Many new moms experience what's called the let-down reflex when they hear a baby's cry or when they think about their newborn. Their breasts start flowing with milk, even when their child is not nursing at that moment! It's as if the mothers have an invisible cord linking them to their child.

In today's verse, God makes it clear that He is even more attentive to you and has more compassion for you than a nursing mother! That although she may forget about you, He never will! He has your name tattooed on His hands.

No matter how neglected, forgotten, or abandoned you may feel by people—including your mother—rest assured that God will never, ever forget you. He is linked to you by the invisible cord of love.

Once more, Lord, You have taken my breath away. No one loves me as much as You do. With You I know I have a true home, now and forever. In You I rest, trust, and find true peace.

I know I'm worthy because God is linked to me by the invisible and everlasting cord of love.

GOD WILL TURN THINGS AROUND FOR YOU

"When you come looking for me, you'll find me. Yes, when you get serious about finding me and want it more than anything else, I'll make sure you won't be disappointed. . . . I'll turn things around for you."
JEREMIAH 29:13–14 MSG

This world is full of distractions. People, events, situations, jobs, media, politics—all these things vie for your attention. And when you get caught up in them, your focus may shift away from God. Before you know it, although you're still routinely doing your devotions, saying brief prayers, and going to church on Sunday, a shift has taken place. You're more caught up in the world than you are in God. You're living your life based on your own wisdom, power, strength, and knowledge.

That's when you need to go looking for God, to desire Him above all other things, including people, events, or the latest news bite. When you do begin seeking God—with all of your heart—you won't be disappointed. On the contrary, He'll start turning things around for you, getting your life and trust in Him back on track—to your good and His glory!

I'm not sure what happened, Lord, but I've gotten so caught up in the world that I have stopped seeking Your wisdom, knowledge, power, and strength. Help me get back on track, God, because my life without You is a dead end.

I know I'm worthy because when I wholeheartedly seek God, He turns things around for me.

GOD MAKES EVERYTHING RIGHT FOR YOU

GOD makes everything come out right; he puts victims back on their feet. . . . GOD's love, though, is ever and always, eternally present to all who fear him, making everything right for them and their children as they follow his Covenant ways and remember to do whatever he said.
PSALM 103:6, 17–18 MSG

• • • • • • • • • • • • • • • • • •

When a little girl falls off her bike, parents are quick to tell her to get right back on. But as she grows, her challenges are greater, making her "falls" a bit more complicated and injurious. Some time may need to pass before she fully recovers and is able to get back up.

God knows you may need time to lick your wounds and rebuild your courage after a breakup, a loss, a rejection, or a physical ailment. So when you're feeling discouraged, thinking you'll never find your soulmate, recover from a loved one's passing, recoup confidence, or regain your physical strength, don't worry. God will make everything come out right in His time. As you're walking with Him, God will rebuild, soothe, and comfort you. Then one day, before you're even aware of it, you'll find yourself back in the saddle, riding along as if you'd never fallen in the first place.

Lord, all the things I'd thought I'd never have or do again are within reach once more. Thank You for Your soothing hand in my life!

I know I'm worthy because God makes everything come out right for me.

GOD KNOWS AND BLESSES YOU

As high as heaven is over the earth, so strong is his love to those who fear him. . . . As parents feel for their children, GOD feels for those who fear him. He knows us inside and out, keeps in mind that we're made of mud.
PSALM 103:11, 13-14 MSG

God loves you more than words can ever express. He—a holy, vast being who is the all-powerful Lord of all—knows you inside and out. He realizes you're made of dust and that your body is a temporal structure. That your thoughts are not as high as His. Yet, because of Jesus, there is no separation from God and His love for you. There is no sin that's confessed that can stand between you and Him.

God is a father more loving, powerful, and wise than any earthly parent. He pardons all your wrongdoing, heals you, pulls you out of the pit, crowns you with love and compassion, and satisfies you with so many good things (see Psalm 103:2-5).

Today, may you know about and bless God as you become more conscious of how much He knows about and blesses you, now and forevermore.

Even with all You know about me, Lord, You love me like no other. Bless the Lord, O my soul, as I seek to know and love Him more and more.

I know I'm worthy because my heavenly loving Father knows and blesses me.

GOD HAS BLESSED YOU WITH DIVINE POWER

His divine power has granted to us everything pertaining to life and godliness, through the true knowledge of Him who called us by His own glory and excellence. Through these He has granted to us His precious and magnificent promises, so that by them you may become partakers of the divine nature.
2 PETER 1:3-4 NASB

Some days you may find yourself uncertain as to what God would have you do or what His plan is for your life. Yet you need not worry. Simply allow Jesus to live His life through you, to understand He's already given you all you need to become more like Him. Jesus is working to teach you how to live a life pleasing to both Him and God the Father.

Jesus has made you promises. One of them is that because you believe in Him, He now lives in you. That means you have a share in His divine nature and that anything is possible. Your job is to keep living in Jesus, listening for His voice, and drinking in His Word. And realize you are a product of love. From Father, to Son, to follower, and back again.

Lord, sometimes I feel like I should be further along in my faith walk. Help me always remember that Jesus is in You, I am in Jesus, and Jesus is in me. So nothing is impossible!

I know I'm worthy because God has made me part of the divine circle!

GOD USES ALL THINGS FOR YOUR GOOD

The king's heart is like channels of water in the hand
of the LORD; He turns it wherever He wishes.
PROVERBS 21:1 NASB

The fact that the Israelites, enslaved by the Egyptians, were growing in number concerned the king of Egypt, so he told the Hebrew midwives to kill any boys that were born. Yet two midwives, who feared God more than Pharaoh, let the boys live!

Thus, the life of Jochebed's baby, Moses, was spared! Three months later, realizing she could no longer hide him, Jochebed put Moses in a basket and set him amid the reeds of the Nile. Moses' sister, Miriam, stood by, waiting to see what would happen.

When Pharaoh's daughter came down to bathe, she saw Moses, pitied him, and sent him to Jochebed to feed until he was weaned. Then the princess raised Moses in her home, allowing him to become well provided for and well educated (see Exodus 1–2). What a great beginning for Moses, whom God would call to free His people from Egypt!

God directs people and situations to work for your good no matter how evil or dire they appear to be. God can turn all things to whatever end He pleases!

Knowing You turn what seems evil and dire to Your own amazing ends
gives me such peace and comfort! All praise and glory to my Lord!

I know I'm worthy because God can turn
all things to His—and my—benefit!

GOD IS NEAR THE CRUSHED AND BROKENHEARTED

The LORD hears his people when they call to him for help.
He rescues them from all their troubles. The LORD is close to
the brokenhearted; he rescues those whose spirits are crushed.
PSALM 34:17–18 NLT

* * * * * * * * * * * * * *

When crushed and brokenhearted, you may find it hard to see through the tears or speak through the sobs. But that's just what you need to do, for God has His eye upon you. He sees what has happened. He longs to give you comfort, courage, and strength. He wants to hold you, to pour His love and attention upon you, to stroke your soul and raise your spirit.

When you are at the lowest of lows, cry out to God for help. Tell Him all about it. He will hear your voice from heaven and respond. God will rescue you from all your troubles. He will draw so close that you won't know where you end and He begins. And then the peace beyond understanding will settle down upon you, and the healing will begin.

It is so good to know that I can come to You and cry upon
Your shoulder, Lord. That You have your eye upon me and are
looking to help and heal me. May Yours be the first comfort I
seek when my heart is breaking and my spirit crushed.

I know I'm worthy because God seeks out, hears, and heals the crushed and brokenhearted.

GOD VIES FOR YOUR ATTENTION

Moses said, I will now turn aside and see this great sight,
why the bush is not burned. And when the Lord saw that he
turned aside to see, God called to him out of the midst of the
bush and said, Moses, Moses! And he said, Here am I.
EXODUS 3:3–4 AMPC

After being raised by Pharaoh's daughter, killing an Egyptian, and fleeing to escape Pharaoh's wrath, Moses became a shepherd in Midian. There he married a priest's daughter and became a father.

Forty years later, Pharaoh died, and Moses was still shepherding his father-in-law's flock, walking a track he'd been down many times before. That's when the Angel of the Lord did something to get his attention. He appeared as a flame in the middle of a bush, yet the bush wasn't destroyed. So Moses turned aside to see this unusual sight. And when God saw him turn, He spoke.

Just as God wanted Moses' attention, He wants yours. He wants to reveal His purpose and path for you. But if you rush by, you'll miss Him. So slow down and keep your eyes open. Look for places where God may be trying to get your attention, and then turn aside from your usual path and listen for the message He has just for you.

I don't want to miss Your message, Lord. So I'm slowing down.
My eyes and ears are open. Speak, Lord. Here I am!

I know I'm worthy because God vies for my attention.

GOD SHAPES AND RESHAPES YOU

*All those people who didn't seem interested in what God was doing
actually embraced what God was doing as he straightened out their
lives. And Israel, who seemed so interested in reading and talking about
what God was doing, missed it. . . . Because instead of trusting God, they
took over. They were absorbed in what they themselves were doing.*
ROMANS 9:30–32 MSG

It is God who made you. He's the potter; you're the lump of clay on His
wheel (see Isaiah 64:8). You're to be pliant, willing to allow God to shape
and reshape you. That means actually spending time with God and in His
Word. Not trying to resist His Spirit's prompts but heeding them. It means
embracing what God's doing in your life and walking where He wills even if
it doesn't make sense to you.

Although you want to serve God, there's danger in becoming like the people
of Israel, who tried to get right with God by following the law and traditions.
"They were so absorbed in their 'God projects' that they didn't notice God
right in front of them" (Romans 9:32 MSG).

Be willing to let God shape and reshape you as He lovingly molds you
into the awesome woman He created you to be.

---

*Lord, I want to be a woman after Your own heart. So I put myself
upon Your wheel. Lovingly shape me, Lord, as You see fit!*

I know I'm worthy because God shapes and reshapes me—for Him.

GOD GIVES YOU TALENTS

"His master replied, 'Well done, good and faithful servant!
You have been faithful with a few things; I will put you in charge
of many things. Come and share your master's happiness! . . .
For whoever has will be given more, and they will have an abundance.'"
MATTHEW 25:21, 29 NIV

Jesus tells a parable about a man who was going on a journey. Before leaving, he entrusted his gold to three servants. To the first, he gave five bags, to the second, two, and to the third, one. When he returned, he went back to his servants to see how they'd fared. The first man with five talents earned his master five more. His master commended him, as he did the second man, who began with two bags and earned two more. But he reprimanded the third man who, through fear, hid his one bag of gold.

The lesson here is that God has gifted you certain abilities and talents. He doesn't want you to bury them because of fear but to use them as you follow Him. And when you do, He'll give you even more to share for His glory!

Speak into my heart, Lord. Reveal the abilities and talents
You want me to use to serve You and help others. Then give
me the courage to use them for Your kingdom and glory.

I know I'm worthy because God has given me talents to use for Him.

GOD FEEDS AND CLOTHES YOU

"Why worry about your clothing? Look at the lilies of the field and how they grow. They don't work or make their clothing, yet Solomon in all his glory was not dressed as beautifully as they are."
MATTHEW 6:28-29 NLT

Jesus uses word pictures to help you understand how to live without anxiety, trusting God for everything, including the basics, what you'll eat, drink, and wear (see Matthew 6:34). Look at the birds. They can't sow or reap, yet God feeds them. And don't worry about what you're to wear. If God adorns the beautiful lily, He'll surely provide you with clothing.

Have no doubt God will feed and clothe you who are so much more valuable to Him than sparrows or flowers. Worrying doesn't add one bit of value to your life. On the contrary, it sucks all the joy out of it.

When you feel anxious, go to God. His love has no limits. It will refresh you like the dew from heaven, making you blossom and sending your roots deep into the soil of His Word (see Hosea 14:4-5), proof of how much He cares for you.

Lord, help me to always remember how much You love, care for, and value me. That You'll see I have all I need and more. I want to live worry-free, knowing Your hand is always overflowing in goodness and provision for me.

I know I'm worthy because God gives me all I need—and more.

GOD IS EAGER FOR YOUR TRUST AND LISTENING EAR

"If you will give earnest heed to the voice of the LORD your God, and do what is right in His sight, and give ear to His commandments, and keep all His statutes, I will put none of the diseases on you which I have put on the Egyptians; for I, the LORD, am your healer."
EXODUS 15:26 NASB

God had performed the miracle of plagues, made the Egyptians so glad to see the Israelites go that they gave them whatever they asked for, opened the Red Sea to allow His people to escape, and closed it to drown their pursuers.

Three days later, the Israelites, thirsting for lack of water, reached Marah. But, its waters being bitter, the people complained to Moses. After Moses cried out to God, God showed Moses a stick and told him to throw it into the water. Moses did, and the water became sweet enough to drink. That's when God told them, "If you listen to me, I won't plague you but heal you."

Only God knows the truth of your circumstances. He's seen what's going to happen next. So instead of rolling out a list of your complaints, stop. Trust God. Open your ears to what He wants you to do, and He'll lead you to abundant water (see Exodus 15:27).

Help me, Lord, to trust and keep my eyes on You, not my circumstances.

I know I'm worthy because God has my trust and listening ear.

GOD PROTECTS YOU WHERE HE DIRECTS YOU

He arose and rebuked the wind and said to the sea,
Hush now! Be still (muzzled)! And the wind ceased (sank
to rest as if exhausted by its beating) and there was
[immediately] a great calm (a perfect peacefulness).
MARK 4:39 AMPC

After preaching all day to a large crowd, Jesus directed the disciples to cross to the other side of the lake. So the disciples started rowing as Jesus fell asleep in the back of the boat. But a terrible storm came up. The high waves were crashing, pouring into the boat, filling it with water. The panicked disciples woke Him, saying, "Master, do You not care that we are perishing?" (Mark 4:38 AMPC).

Jesus got up and rebuked the wind, and suddenly it stopped and there was a wonderful calm. Then He turned to the disciples, asking, "Why are you so timid *and* fearful? How is it that you have no faith (no firmly relying trust)?" (Mark 4:40 AMPC).

When storms assail you, turn to Jesus—not in a faithless panic but with the assurance that Jesus is in your boat and will protect you wherever He's directed you to go. You will make it to the other side!

Jesus, thank You for riding through good days and bad
with me. I trust You to see me safely through all my crossings!

I know I'm worthy because Jesus protects me wherever He directs me.

GOD GIVES YOU CREATIVE POWER

Do not neglect the gift which is in you. . .which was directly imparted to you [by the Holy Spirit]. . . . Practice and cultivate and meditate upon these duties; throw yourself wholly into them [as your ministry], so that your progress may be evident to everybody.
1 TIMOTHY 4:14–15 AMPC

Everything in the heavens and on the earth—seen and unseen—was created by God, the Master Creator, through Jesus (see Colossians 1:16–17). And because you were made in God's image (see Genesis 1:27), you have been endowed with creative abilities.

Then, when you accepted Jesus, the Holy Spirit gave you special spiritual gifts. Those gifts may be teaching, preaching, writing, encouraging, singing, painting, organizing, hospitality. . .you name it! All to help extend and build up God's kingdom.

Don't neglect that special gift that only you can use to help others. Find out what it is then throw yourself into using your particular ability, making it a ministry that will make this world a better place—and give you joy as you serve your Master Creator. We're all waiting!

Thank You, Lord, for giving me creative power. Lead me to what that gift is and how I can hone it. Then show me how You would like me to use it for Your kingdom and glory—and my joy!

I know I'm worthy because God gives me creative power and gifts to use for His glory and my joy.

GOD MADE A BRAND-NEW YOU

Therefore if any person is [ingrafted] in Christ (the Messiah) he is a new creation (a new creature altogether); the old [previous moral and spiritual condition] has passed away. Behold, the fresh and new has come!
2 CORINTHIANS 5:17 AMPC

Jesus has saved you! You are now washed of sins, are living an eternal life, and participate in Christ's divine nature. The old you—who you were before you knew and accepted Christ—is now gone. Your old beliefs, fears, plans, loves, value system, and priorities are gone. You see things a new way—through Christ's eyes. And the Holy Spirit is on hand to help direct, steer, comfort, inspire, and prompt you to live in and for Christ, following His direction, lead, and path.

God made you a brand-new person, one who treasures the things of heaven instead of the things of the earth. You're no longer a material girl but a spiritual woman who God values above all other things. Praise God for your new start in this eternal life!

I am so happy that You have saved me, Jesus. That I have the Spirit to help me. That because of You, God sees me as a new creature, holy and perfect. Help me live this life Your way.

I know I'm worthy because God has made me a brand-new woman!

GOD GIVES YOU DISCERNMENT

Don't let anyone divert you from the truth. It's the person
who acts right who is right, just as we see it lived out in our
righteous Messiah. Those who make a practice of sin are
straight from the Devil, the pioneer in the practice of sin.
The Son of God entered the scene to abolish the Devil's ways.
1 JOHN 3:7–8 MSG

Sometimes it's hard to tell who the "good guys" are in this world. But through
the apostle John, God gives you guidance in this area so you won't be led
astray by people who aren't living the "right" (righteous) way. Although some
people seem to talk a good game, if they're not practicing what they teach
but are habitually sinning, they're not walking in the light. And if they're not
walking in the light, they're walking in the dark with the devil. So neither
follow these "bad guys" nor take their words as gospel.

The "good guys" are the ones living the right way, following Jesus' example. They truly reflect Jesus' light, having taken on His divine nature and
manifesting the power of His life in them. The good guys are the ones whose
example you'll want to emulate as God continues to build up your faith and
life in Christ.

Thank You, Lord, for giving me a litmus test so I won't be led astray!

I know I'm worthy because God helps me discern the good from the bad.

GOD VALUES AND BLESSES YOUR SERVANT'S HEART

*"If I then, the Lord and the Teacher, washed your feet,
you also ought to wash one another's feet. For I gave you
an example that you also should do as I did to you. . . .
If you know these things, you are blessed if you do them."*
JOHN 13:14–15, 17 NASB

Imagine living in a society where, before you sat down for a meal, good hosts made sure a non-Jewish slave washed your feet, dusty from your travels on the road. Now imagine being Jesus' disciple. You're in the middle of dinner and the Son of God gets up, takes off His coat, ties a towel around His waist, pours water in a basin, and begins to wash your dirty, stinky feet!

How astounding, unusual, against the norm—but that was Jesus! By washing the feet of His followers—including Judas, who would later betray Him—He demonstrated how believers were to be humble and serve others. It also pointed to how Jesus' death would wash away their sins.

Be as Jesus. Be humble and have a servant's heart, not judging who you should minister to. If you do these things, God will bless you.

Show me, Lord, who I can humbly serve as I walk Your way today.

I know I'm worthy because God blesses my humble, servant's heart.

GOD HELPS YOU UNDERSTAND

But there is a spirit within people, the breath of the Almighty within them, that makes them intelligent.
JOB 32:8 NLT

When God created humankind, He breathed the breath of life into them (see Genesis 2:7). That breath gave them not only a life force but also intelligence. Proverbs 2:6-8 says from God's mouth (from which He speaks and exhales breath) come knowledge, understanding, and all the wisdom you need to live a godly life. This treasure is a shield to all those who walk with Him.

Jesus breathed the Holy Spirit onto the disciples, who were hiding in the upper room after His resurrection (see John 20:22). He did that to give them a taste of what they'd receive when the Holy Spirit would be given to live within them at Pentecost.

As a believer, you have the breath of God within you. You've been given wisdom from above in the form of the Holy Spirit. Why? Because you're precious to God, and He wants you to have His wisdom, all you need to stay on His path!

Got a problem? Can't understand something? Go to God. He has all the wisdom, intelligence, and knowledge you need—and so much more.

Thank You, Lord, for giving me wisdom when I'm stymied, confused, or uncertain of which way to go, what to do. With Your breath upon me and Your Spirit within me, I know I'll find my way.

I know I'm worthy because God has breathed
His wisdom and Spirit upon me!

GOD WORKS MIRACLES IN YOUR LIFE

This, the first of His signs (miracles, wonderworks), Jesus performed in Cana of Galilee, and manifested His glory [by it He displayed His greatness and His power openly], and His disciples believed in Him [adhered to, trusted in, and relied on Him].

JOHN 2:11 AMPC

Through people and other tools, God worked many miracles in the Old Testament. He parted waters, healed lepers, supplied an abundance of oil for a poor widow, crumbled walls at the sound of trumpets and shouts, brought water gushing out of a rock, and much more.

Then when Jesus arrived, He also displayed His power. He healed many people, chased out demons, calmed the wind, smoothed over the sea, turned water into wine in Cana, raised the dead, and multiplied loaves and fishes to feed crowds of thousands! Later, Jesus' followers performed many miracles in His name!

When you need a miracle, pray for God's help. Don't tell Him what you want Him to do and how you want Him to do it. Just put yourself and your situation in Jesus' hands, and open your eyes of faith so you will see His "sign" when it comes—proof of His eternal, miracle-working power!

Lord, I am putting myself and my circumstances in Your worthy hands. Work Your miracle, Lord, and give me the eyes of faith so I can see it and praise You!

I know I'm worthy because God works miracles in my life!

GOD EMPATHIZES WITH YOU

In all their affliction He was afflicted, and the Angel of His presence saved them; in His love and in His pity He redeemed them; and He lifted them up and carried them all the days of old.

ISAIAH 63:9 AMPC

There's nothing you've gone through that Jesus hasn't already experienced. He's been beaten, rejected, abused, mocked, whipped, cursed, abandoned, betrayed, despised, and tortuously hung on a cross. Even now, people use His very name, the one you revere, as a curse. They continue to mock and reject Him.

Yet Jesus never once stopped following God's will for His life. Even though He was homeless, with no place to lay His head, He never once deviated from God's path. The night before He died, Jesus "began to show grief *and* distress of mind and was deeply depressed" (Matthew 26:37 AMPC). And still He prayed, "Nevertheless, not what I will [not what I desire], but as You will *and* desire" (Matthew 26:39 AMPC).

Jesus knows what you're going through. He and the angel of His presence have saved you because He loves and pities you. He has compassion for you. So when the going gets tough, go to Jesus. Allow Him to lift you up and carry you His way.

Lift me up, Lord. Carry me to the peace of Your presence as I live Your way.

I know I'm worthy because God carries me when the going gets tough.

GOD CALLS YOU A CHILD OF THE MOST HIGH

"But love your enemies, do good to them, and lend to them without expecting to get anything back. Then your reward will be great, and you will be children of the Most High, because he is kind to the ungrateful and wicked."

LUKE 6:35 NIV

Jesus loved turning the world on its ears! In Matthew 5:43, He reminded the people that they'd heard it said that they should "Love your neighbor," a quote from the law of Moses (Leviticus 19:18). But to that He added the scribes' and Pharisees' interpretation and application of that command: "and hate your enemy."

Fortunately, Jesus came to clarify lots of things, including the idea that you're *not* to hate your enemies but *love* them! Do them good, give them things without expecting anything in return, for when you do, you'll be acting just like your Father and be called His daughter! That's because, time and time again, God is kind to those who are not just unthankful but evil. So, like Father, like daughter.

Today show God that you value Him as much as He values you, by loving an enemy. Doing so comes with a wonderful reward!

Lord of all, show me how to bless and love my enemies.
Then give me the means to do so—for You!

I kow I'm worthy because I am a daughter of the Most High!

GOD SENDS MESSENGERS TO KEEP YOU SAFE

An angel of the Lord appeared to Joseph in a dream.
"Get up! Flee to Egypt with the child and his mother,"
the angel said. "Stay there until I tell you to return."
MATTHEW 2:13 NLT

God sends you messages by circumstances, the Word, pastors, angels, and regular people.

For Joseph, the foster father of Jesus, messages came from a dream angel. The first told him not to send away but to marry his wife-to-be, an already-pregnant Mary. Joseph obeyed (see Matthew 1:19–24).

Later, wise men visiting Jesus were warned by a dream angel not to stop at Herod's place and tell him where they'd found the Boy-King. So they went home another way (see Matthew 2:12). When the wise men left, Joseph was warned by a dream angel to take Jesus to Egypt so Herod wouldn't kill Him (see Matthew 2:13). Joseph obeyed. Later a dream angel told Joseph that those seeking to kill Jesus had died, and it was now safe to go back to Israel (see Matthew 2:19–21). So Joseph did. Then, warned of danger by God in a dream, Joseph headed to Galilee and stopped in Nazareth (see Matthew 2:22–23).

There's a pattern here. When you get a warning from God or one of His personal messengers, don't just hear it—heed it. He'll keep you safe.

Lord, I want to play it safe. Open my
ears and eyes to hear Your messages.

I know I'm worthy because God sends messengers to keep me safe!

GOD GIVES YOU JESUS— YOUR MANNA FOR LIFE

"Your ancestors ate manna in the wilderness, but they all died.
Anyone who eats the bread from heaven, however, will never die.
I am the living bread that came down from heaven. Anyone who eats
this bread will live forever; and this bread, which I will offer. . .is my flesh."
JOHN 6:49–51 NLT

When the Israelites began their wilderness wandering, they began to hunger. They grumbled to Moses, "If only the LORD had killed us back in Egypt. . . . There we sat around pots filled with meat and ate all the bread we wanted. But now you have brought us into this wilderness to starve us all to death" (Exodus 16:3 NLT). So God rained down bread from heaven, something the Israelites had never seen before. They called it *manna*, meaning, "What is it?" (Exodus 16:15 NLT). Yet this manna was temporary, a small foreshadowing of what Jesus would provide.

When Jesus came, He said *He* was the bread God gave from heaven and that all who ate this bread would never die! Jesus offered His body, His flesh, on the cross so you could live forever. With Jesus, the Bread of Life, you have all the nourishment you'll ever need. All you require comes from and is found in Him—your manna for life!

Thank You, God, for giving me all I need to live—in Jesus!

I know I'm worthy because God has supplied me manna for life!

GOD GOES THE DISTANCE FOR YOU

The king's officer pleaded with Him, Sir, do come down at once before my little child is dead! Jesus answered him, Go in peace; your son will live! And the man put his trust in what Jesus said and started home.
JOHN 4:49–50 AMPC

Jesus was in Cana when a Roman official begged Him to come with him to Capernaum. It was there, a sixteen-mile journey, where his son lay dying. Jesus told the officer to go in peace and that his son would live. Trusting Jesus at His word, the man started the journey back home. But while he was on his way, his servants met up with him and told him, "Your son lives!" (John 4:51 AMPC). When the official asked when the boy had begun to get better, they named the same hour that Jesus had said to him, "Your son will live" (John 4:53 AMPC).

There is no distance God will not cover to answer your prayer when you trust in Him for the results. Today, ask God for help, trust God at His word, then go in peace knowing He will go the distance to answer your prayer!

You've proven time and time again, Lord, that You will go the distance for me when I ask You for help and take You at Your word. Today, I go in peace, knowing You hear and will answer my prayer!

I know I'm worthy because God goes the distance for me!

GOD IS YOUR FOREVER COMPANION

The people said, "You aren't even fifty years old. How can you say you have seen Abraham?" Jesus answered, "I tell you the truth, before Abraham was even born, I AM!"
JOHN 8:57-58 NLT

When God appeared to Moses in the burning bush, Moses asked Him what His name was. Moses wanted to be able to tell the people who this talking flame was in case they asked him. That's when God told Moses, "I AM WHO I AM. Say this to the people of Israel: I AM has sent me to you" (Exodus 3:14 NLT). The Hebrew phrase "I AM WHO I AM" can also be translated as "I WILL BE WHAT I WILL BE." This reflects back to Exodus 3:12 (NLT), where God tells Moses, "I will be with you." God said He would be with Moses to fulfill his calling.

Now here is Jesus, thousands of years later, telling people that *He* is the I AM, the eternal one, that He was around before Abraham was even born! That means God and Jesus always have been, always are, and always will be. They are your forever companions, there to aid, love, provide for, and give you hope wherever and whenever you need them—all the years of your life and beyond!

It's hard to grasp how eternal You are, Lord. But I'm so grateful for Your forever presence as we walk this road together!

I know I'm worthy because God is my forever companion!

GOD GIVES YOU COURAGE—
JUST WHEN YOU NEED IT

Joseph, he of Arimathea, noble and honorable in rank and a respected member of the council (Sanhedrin), who was himself waiting for the kingdom of God, daring the consequences, took courage and ventured to go to Pilate and asked for the body of Jesus.
MARK 15:43 AMPC

Joseph of Arimathea, mentioned in all four gospels (see Matthew 27:57–60; Mark 15:43–46; Luke 23:50–54; John 19:38–41), was a rich and respected Jewish leader. He was also one of the few who hadn't agreed with the decisions and actions of the other religious leaders (see Luke 23:51). In fact, Joseph had actually been a disciple of Jesus, but he kept that secret because he feared the Jews (see John 19:38).

Yet God gave Joseph the courage to ask Pilate for permission to take down Jesus' body. Then Joseph took it away and worked with Nicodemus to wrap Jesus' body with the spices and place it in a new tomb carved out of rock.

God gives those He loves and values the courage to do what He prompts them to do—regardless of the consequences. You too will be given the same courage, just when you need it.

You know the things I'm afraid to do, Lord. Give me the courage, just as You did Joseph, to dare to do what You're calling me to do, in Jesus' name. Amen.

I know I'm worthy because God gives me courage—just when I need it.

146

GOD REALIGNS YOUR VALUES

"Don't store up treasures here on earth, where moths eat them and rust destroys them, and where thieves break in and steal. Store your treasures in heaven, where moths and rust cannot destroy, and thieves do not break in and steal. Wherever your treasure is, there the desires of your heart will also be."
MATTHEW 6:19–21 NLT

Jesus presents you with a choice. You can either be focused on the things of this earth or—and it's a big "OR"—you can be focused on the things of heaven. It's a choice between having your heart set on living for and loving creation or living for and loving the Creator. The treasures on the earth will eventually fade to nothing or be stolen, but the treasures in heaven are indestructible and safe from thieves.

Jesus makes it clearer in Luke 16:13 (AMPC) where He says, "You cannot serve God and mammon (riches, or anything in which you trust and on which you rely)."

When you follow Jesus, God helps you realign your values. He urges you to trust, serve, and rely on Him alone. He asks that you place your focus and desire on valuing and treasuring Him and His will only, realizing He alone is sufficient for all you need or want. He wants the best path for you.

Lord, help me reevaluate what I think is important in this life. Show me where my heart is, and help me get better aligned with You.

I know I'm worthy because God puts me on a better path.

GOD KEEPS YOU FROM STUMBLING IN THE DARK

*Then Jesus again spoke to them, saying, "I am the
Light of the world; he who follows Me will not walk
in the darkness, but will have the Light of life."*
JOHN 8:12 NASB

Jesus is the Light of the World. He's the light the psalmist wrote about: "Light, space, zest—that's GOD! So, with him on my side I'm fearless, afraid of no one and nothing" (Psalm 27:1 MSG). He's the great light that would be seen by the people who live in darkness, the light that would guide the nations and restore the people of Israel (see Isaiah 9:2; 42:6). He's the light for the Gentiles, extending God's salvation to the end of the earth (see Isaiah 49:6).

As a follower of Jesus, you're in the light and are now to walk as "children of Light" (Ephesians 5:8 AMPC). That means being kind, being good, being upright, doing what is pleasing to God, and having no part in the darkness. "God is Light, and there is no darkness in Him at all" (1 John 1:5 AMPC).

Each day look for the light of God. Allow it to shine within and be a beam upon your path. Doing so will keep you from stumbling in the dark.

*God, thank You for being the light of my life. Shine Your light
within so I can better reflect Your presence in my life.*

I know I'm worthy because God keeps me in the light.

GOD GIVES YOU THE SPIRIT OF LIVING WATER

"Let anyone who is thirsty come to me and drink. Whoever believes in me, as Scripture has said, rivers of living water will flow from within them." By this he meant the Spirit, whom those who believed in him were later to receive.

JOHN 7:37–39 NIV

Jesus is the conduit to the rivers of living water. Those who followed Him received a helper that came after Jesus went back to heaven so that they would not be left alone. And it's this helper, the Holy Spirit, who's the living water you now have within you. That Spirit cools you down, quenches the thirst for God, and gives you the energy you need to live a godly life. As you drink Him in, you find the godly wisdom you need, His comfort, direction, guidance, and help.

In Isaiah 55:1 (NIV), Isaiah wrote, "Come, all you who are thirsty, come to the waters; and you who have no money, come, buy and eat! Come. . . without money and without cost." Jesus is inviting you to freely partake of what your soul needs and craves—He who is the rock that gushes out water for the thirsty walking in a dry and weary land.

Lord, I'm thirsting for the comfort and free-flowing blessings from the Spirit within. Nothing else will satisfy. So I come and drink.

I know I'm worthy because God has gifted me with the Spirit of living water.

GOD GAVE YOU THE LORD OF PEACE

Now may the Lord of peace Himself grant you His peace (the peace of His kingdom) at all times and in all ways [under all circumstances and conditions, whatever comes]. The Lord [be] with you all.

2 THESSALONIANS 3:16 AMPC

When Jesus was here on the earth, living the human experience, along with the joy He endured many trials. He was accused of something He didn't do and then was crucified for it. He was beaten, laughed at, mocked, betrayed, abandoned, whipped, and stabbed with a spear. Yet through all of these troubles, He kept the peace of God.

Jesus knows everything you're going through. He's experienced every emotion you're feeling. And He's walking every step of the way with you, for He has promised to never leave or forsake you.

Today, ask Jesus to give you His peace at all times and under every circumstance. He is there for you day and night. Lean back upon His chest, feel His breath, absorb all the light and love He has to give. His kingdom peace is yours for the taking.

Jesus, I need Your peace each and every day. As I come into Your presence, shower me with the calm that only You can provide. Soothe my nerves, give me hope, allow me to rest in Your arms until I have the peace that is beyond understanding.

I know I'm worthy because God has given me the Lord of Peace.

GOD WANTS YOU TO BREAK THE GOOD NEWS

How beautiful on the mountains are the feet of the messenger bringing good news, breaking the news that all's well, proclaiming good times, announcing salvation, telling Zion, "Your God reigns!"
ISAIAH 52:7 MSG

When you think about feet, the word *beautiful* may not be the first one that pops into your mind. Yet beautiful are the feet of those who carry the message of God's good news—that Jesus saves and loves you!

Amazingly enough, the first person to spread the news of Jesus' triumph over death was a woman! When Mary Magdalene went to the tomb looking for Jesus' body, she heard a voice behind her. It was her beloved Jesus saying her name—Mary! She fell down and worshipped Him. But Jesus told her to go and tell the disciples He was going to ascend to Father God. And so she did (see John 20:1–18).

God wants you to tell others about Jesus (see Matthew 28:16–20), what He's done for all people, and what He's done for you. When you do, you too will have beautiful feet!

I am honored that You want to use me to spread the good news, Lord. Give me the right words to say to others at the right time. And as I do so, may I be as thrilled as Mary at the tomb.

I know I'm worthy because God wants me to break the good news!

GOD SEEKS THE BEST IN YOU

*Jesus said to him, "Today salvation has come to
this house, because this man, too, is a son of Abraham.
For the Son of Man came to seek and to save the lost."*
LUKE 19:9–10 NIV

Zacchaeus was the chief tax collector in the Jericho region. When Jesus was passing through town, Zacchaeus, short in stature, couldn't see Him, so he ran ahead of the crowd and climbed up a sycamore tree.

When Jesus came near Zacchaeus' observation post, He looked up and said to him, "Zacchaeus, come down immediately. I must stay at your house today" (Luke 19:5 NIV). Thrilled, the little man shimmied down the tree and welcomed Jesus to his home. Yet people began to make snide comments, such as "He has gone to be the guest of a sinner" (Luke 19:7 NIV). And in that moment, Zacchaeus told Jesus he would immediately give half his possessions to the poor and pay back four times the amount he'd cheated others.

After Jesus enters your heart and you begin to know Him more intimately, you find yourself willingly and ably reforming yourself and your life, doing things you could never do on your own. And as you continue your walk, God continues to seek the best you—to your joy and His glory!

*Jesus, thank You for bringing Your light to my life. Thank
You for seeking out and saving me, making me a better
and more joyful servant to and friend of You!*

I know I'm worthy because God seeks the best in me!

GOD MAKES ALL THINGS CLEAR TO YOU

The woman said to Him, I know that Messiah is coming, He Who
is called the Christ (the Anointed One); and when He arrives,
He will tell us everything we need to know and make it clear
to us. Jesus said to her, I Who now speak with you am He.
JOHN 4:25–26 AMPC

Long ago God spoke to His people through prophets. But when Jesus arrived, God spoke through Him (see Hebrews 1:1-2). Jesus tells you everything you need to know. He makes all things clear.

God sent Jesus so you would get to know and understand Him. He wants you to search His Word so that you can find all the blessings He offers.

Allow Jesus to speak to you. Rediscover His parables, and take to heart each one's lesson. Be conscious of the Holy Spirit's translation of God's Word. Trust that He'll point you to the scriptures you personally need to hear. Keep your heart open to God's will and way through prayer and praise. In so doing, you'll better home in on God's purpose for your life.

Rest easy. "For God is not a God of confusion but of peace" (1 Corinthians 14:33 NASB). He'll help you sort things out.

I realize, Lord, that You're the answer to all my questions.
And although You won't tell me everything, You'll tell
me all I need to know. This alone gives me peace.

I know I'm worthy because God makes all things clear to me.

GOD USES YOUR FAITH TO MAKE THINGS HAPPEN

Jesus said to them, Do you believe that I am able to do this?
They said to Him, Yes, Lord. Then He touched their eyes, saying,
According to your faith and trust and reliance [on the power
invested in Me] be it done to you; and their eyes were opened.
MATTHEW 9:28–30 AMPC

∙ ∙ ∙ ∙ ∙ ∙ ∙ ∙ ∙ ∙ ∙ ∙ ∙ ∙

Two blind men began following Jesus, crying out for His mercy. So Jesus asked them, "Do you think I'm able to do this?" They answered yes, prompting Jesus to touch their eyes, saying, "Because of your faith, it will happen" (Matthew 9:29 NLT). And they regained their sight!

Later, Jesus was in His hometown of Nazareth, teaching in the synagogue there. Yet "because of their unbelief, he couldn't do any miracles among them except to place his hands on a few sick people and heal them" (Mark 6:5 NLT; see also Matthew 13:58). It's not that Jesus couldn't do any miracles there, but that He didn't have the will to do them because the people rejected Him. The wonders Jesus works belong only to people who believe or are ready to believe in Him and His power.

God loves you and wants to work miracles in your life. And He will do so according to your faith!

I believe in You, Lord! I trust in Your power.
Work a wonder in my life, in Jesus' name. Amen!

I know I'm worthy because God uses my faith to work His wonders.

GOD TURNS YOUR NEGATIVES INTO POSITIVES

We are destroying speculations and every lofty thing raised up against the knowledge of God, and we are taking every thought captive to the obedience of Christ.

2 CORINTHIANS 10:5 NASB

God can take every negative thought you have and make it a positive. When you think you cannot do the impossible, Jesus tells you, "If you had faith even as small as a mustard seed, you could say to this mountain, 'Move from here to there,' and it would move. Nothing would be impossible" (Matthew 17:20 NLT). When you think no one loves you, God says He does (see Zephaniah 3:17). When you think you don't have the strength, God says you can do all things through Christ who gives you strength (see Philippians 4:13). When you think you'll never get rid of your burden or that no one cares about you, Jesus tells you to cast your burden on Him; He'll carry it because *He* cares for you (see 1 Peter 5:7).

Make it a habit to take every negative thought to Christ. Then allow God to transform you, giving you a positive thought—filled with His truth—to fix firmly in your mind.

Lord, please make me more aware of what I'm thinking. And if any negative thoughts come up, prompt me to take them to Christ and replace them with Your truth! Transform me, Lord!

I know I'm worthy because God turns my negative thoughts into positives.

GOD WILL CONTINUALLY GUIDE AND RESTORE YOU

Feed the hungry, and help those in trouble. Then your light will shine out from the darkness, and the darkness around you will be as bright as noon. The LORD will guide you continually, giving you water when you are dry and restoring your strength.

ISAIAH 58:10–11 NLT

God doesn't want you to live merely to satisfy your desires. If you have truly accepted Christ, you'll want to do for others: to work with the homeless, help in a soup kitchen, aid a blood drive, cook meals for the aged or widowed, or make a prayer shawl for the injured, ill, or dying.

When you serve others as Jesus served you, God promises you'll shine bright. And God will give you continual guidance, quench your thirst and hunger, and restore your strength. As you bless, God will bless you and your efforts over and over again! You are a precious one who is walking in His light, taking care of those precious to Him who can no longer take care of themselves. It's a three-way win!

I want to serve You by serving others, Lord. Show me what You would have me do and who You want me to serve. I know You'll give me all the resources and strength to do whatever task You put upon my heart.

I know I'm worthy because God promises to continually guide me and restore my strength!

GOD WANTS YOU TO SEEK HIM EARLY

I love those who love me, and those who seek me early and diligently shall find me.... For whoever finds me [Wisdom] finds life and draws forth and obtains favor from the Lord.

God wants to be in on everything you're thinking about and planning. He wants you to come to Him so He can help, guide, inspire, and provide you with all the resources you'll need. And the best time of day for you to come to Him is in the early morning hours, before the rest of the house awakes, before the dog needs to be let out, before the cat needs to be fed, and before your thoughts start running wild, doubts of your ability creep in, or fear rears its head.

Begin your day with God. Seek His face. Peruse His Word. And most important of all, pray. Pray for every need you have, every task before you, every person you'll encounter, every desire you'd like Him to bless. As you seek God, you'll find Him. Have no doubt about that. He'll give you the wisdom, peace, strength, energy, and resources you need today and every day.

Lord, thank You for spending time with me. Here's how my day looks.... Please bless my efforts and give me all I need as I live in You.

I know I'm worthy because God wants me to seek—and find—Him!

GOD'S ANGEL SURROUNDS, GUARDS, AND RESCUES YOU

This poor man cried, and the Lord heard him, and saved him out of all his troubles. The Angel of the Lord encamps around those who fear Him [who revere and worship Him with awe] and each of them He delivers.
PSALM 34:6–7 AMPC

When you are in trouble, when you are desperate, when you see no way out, cry to God. Pray for His help. And Yahweh Himself—the most powerful of all beings—will rescue you, deliver you from all that's coming against you. Yahweh—the one who parts waters, rules the universe, calms storms, battles armies, and has control over all forces seen and unseen—will surround you with His presence, with all His strength, power, and energy.

God will set up a circle of protection around you so that nothing will reach you or harm you. Why? Because you, whom He loves, cried out to Him. Like a loving father who will do anything to protect His little one, God the Father is ready to put everything on the line to get you out of whatever straits you are in. Just call, and Yahweh will be there.

I stand amazed, Lord, at the lengths You, the all-powerful one, will go to when I find myself in a desperate situation, at the power You'll so willingly expend on my behalf. Thank You, Lord, for loving me so much!

I know I'm worthy because Yahweh surrounds, guards, and rescues me.

GOD, YOUR ABBA, HAS ADOPTED YOU

God sent him to buy freedom for us who were slaves to the law, so that he could adopt us as his very own children. And because we are his children, God has sent the Spirit of his Son into our hearts, prompting us to call out, "Abba, Father." Now you are. . .God's own child. . . . [H]is heir.
GALATIANS 4:5–7 NLT

* * * * * * * * * * * * * *

When Jesus died for you, allowing you to be forgiven your mistakes, you automatically became a part of God's forever family. Because the almighty Lord has adopted you as His very own little girl, He has sent the Spirit of Jesus into your heart. You are now the heir to His promises and have access to "every spiritual blessing in the heavenly realms" (Ephesians 1:3 NLT). When you realize all these blessings and benefits, you can't help but call out, "Abba, Father."

Abba is the Aramaic term that can be translated as *Daddy*. It suggests that God wants to be close to you, to have a lasting intimate relationship with you.

Feel Abba's Spirit deep within you. Snuggle up to His warmth and compassion. Delight in His presence as He reaches out to embrace you in His arms of love.

Abba! Daddy God! Thank You for adopting me. My heart is full of joy. I want to jump into Your arms. Hold me, Abba. Keep me close.

I know I'm worthy because Abba, God, has adopted me as His very own daughter.

GOD'S WORD GIVES YOU SUPERNATURAL INSIGHT

You, through Your commandments, make me wiser than my enemies, for [Your words] are ever before me.
PSALM 119:98 AMPC

• • • • • • • • • • • • • • • • • •

When Solomon became king, God appeared to him in a dream and asked, "What do you want? Ask, and I will give it to you!" (1 Kings 3:5 NLT). Solomon explained that even though he was king, he was still a child who didn't know his way around. So he asked God to give him an understanding heart so he could rule His people well. God was so pleased with this answer that He gave Solomon not only wisdom but riches and fame! Later, Solomon penned these words: "Getting wisdom is the wisest thing you can do!" (Proverbs 4:7 NLT).

Your greatest source for wisdom is found in God's Word. As you read, study, and meditate upon it, you'll gain more understanding and deeper insight than your teachers and elders. It will also keep you on God's good path (see Psalm 119:98–102). Whatever you do, "Don't turn your back on wisdom, for she will protect you. Love her, and she will guard you" (Proverbs 4:6 NLT).

I want and need the wisdom and supernatural insight that only You can provide, Lord. Show me where You would have me start my search within Your Word. Lead me by Your Spirit.

I know I'm worthy because God has supplied me with supernatural insight through His Word.

GOD WILL NEVER DISAPPOINT YOU

The LORD answered me and said, "Record the vision and inscribe it on tablets, that the one who reads it may run. For the vision is yet for the appointed time; it hastens toward the goal and it will not fail. Though it tarries, wait for it; for it will certainly come, it will not delay."

HABAKKUK 2:2–3 NASB

When you've poured out your heart to God and asked Him for a vision, an answer, a plan, He wants you to be patient as you await the answer He'll provide by His Word, Spirit, or providence. He won't disappoint you or your expectations when you patiently wait to hear from Him or see evidence of His answer. Though your blessing may take a long while in reaching you, it will finally come, and its timing will be perfect.

Simeon was a devout Jew, waiting for and expecting the Messiah. The Holy Spirit had told him he would not die before he'd seen the Chosen One. One day, God prompted him to go to the temple. And that's where and when Simeon met Jesus, calling Him "a light to reveal God to the nations" (Luke 2:32 NLT).

Be patient in God. He won't disappoint you.

I'm keeping the faith, Lord, patiently waiting for and expecting a word, a sign, an answer from You. I know Your timing will be perfect.

I know I'm worthy because God will never disappoint me.

GOD GIVES YOU RESISTANCE

So be subject to God. Resist the devil [stand firm against him], and he will flee from you. Come close to God and He will come close to you.
JAMES 4:7–8 AMPC

• • • • • • • • • • • • • • • •

The Bible makes it clear that you cannot serve two masters, both God and mammon (see Matthew 6:24). You cannot be a friend of the world and of God at the same time (see James 4:4). The apostle John explains why: "For the world offers only a craving for physical pleasure, a craving for everything we see, and pride in our achievements and possessions. These are not from the Father, but are from this world" (1 John 2:16 NLT). And all things worldly are transient, temporal, and fading. "But anyone who does what pleases God will live forever" (1 John 2:17 NLT).

When you choose submitting to God instead of the world, you can stand firm against the evil one. He'll flee from you. As God works His will in you, you'll be able to shout no to the devil, and he'll take off. A mere whisper of yes to God will bring Him running to your side. The best route, the eternal road, is with God. For as you "humble yourselves before the Lord. . .he will lift you up in honor" (James 4:10 NLT).

Lord, I don't want to be double-minded. Help me to stay humble, to follow Your plan and path. I want to please You alone.

I know I'm worthy because God helps me resist lies and darkness.

GOD OFFERS HEALING

When Jesus noticed him lying there [helpless], knowing that he had
already been a long time in that condition, He said to him, Do you
want to become well? [Are you really in earnest about getting well?]
JOHN 5:6 AMPC

Jesus went to the Bethesda pool where many sick, blind, and lame people lay, waiting for an angel of the Lord to stir up the water. Those who were first to go into the water were afterward healed from their affliction.

By that pool was a man who'd been sick for thirty-eight years. Seeing him lying there, Jesus asked him, "Do you want to get well?" The man said he couldn't get well because he had no one to help him get into the water in time. So Jesus simply told him to stand up, pick up his mat, and walk. At His words, the man was healed instantly.

There may be times when you get so attached to an ailment, habit, or problem that it becomes a part of your life. You can't seem to let it go and let God handle it. Yet God offers you total healing of all your ills. When you allow yourself to "let go and let God," He will make you whole. He'd never do anything less.

I know I have some problems and worries that I've not
been letting You handle, Lord. No more excuses. I turn
myself completely over to You. Make me whole.

I know I'm worthy because God offers me healing.

GOD WANTS YOU TO BE HIS HANDS AND FEET

Now you [collectively] are Christ's body and [individually]
you are members of it, each part severally and distinct
[each with his own place and function].
1 CORINTHIANS 12:27 AMPC

You have a particular talent, spiritual gift, ability that God wants you to use to serve others. He wants you to be His hands and feet in this world, allowing Him to serve and help others *through you* (see 1 Peter 4:10).

You're a unique woman, God's masterpiece. You've been created new in Christ Jesus. And God has given you a special assignment, a purpose only you can live out. Long ago He made plans to have you be here in this time and place to answer His call, do His will, and act as His hands and feet (see Ephesians 2:10).

Do not doubt that you can do what you've been called to do. For God has prepared you for every good work (see 2 Timothy 3:17). It's all been prearranged by Him. Everything is in place. Pray that God would reveal His mission for you, show you the steps to take, reveal the work ahead. Then walk in His will and way with all the confidence a daughter of the King should have.

Lord, I'm ready. Reveal the gift You want me to use to serve
You, to be Your heavenly hands and feet on this earth.

I know I'm worthy because God wants me to be His hands and feet.

GOD WILL STRAIGHTEN YOU OUT

There was a woman there who for eighteen years had had an infirmity caused by a spirit (a demon of sickness). She was bent completely forward and utterly unable to straighten herself up or to look upward.
LUKE 13:11 AMPC

Jesus was teaching in a synagogue. It was there he saw a woman who'd been crippled by an evil spirit. For eighteen years she was bent over double. There was nothing she could do to straighten herself up or to even look up! So Jesus called her over, saying, "Woman, you are released from your infirmity!" (Luke 13:12 AMPC). He then laid His hands on her, and she was instantly straight! Right away "she recognized. . .and praised God" (Luke 13:13 AMPC).

There will be times when you cannot lift yourself up or straighten yourself out no matter how hard you try. That's when you need to seek out Jesus to release you from whatever has bent you over. One word from Him and you're made right again, able to once more look up and praise God. Seek out Jesus. And the combination of your faith and God's restorative power will heal whatever ails you, straighten out whatever you cannot, prompting you to look up and praise the master healer.

There is something I cannot do in my own power, Lord. So I bring my faith and my malady to You, ready for Your healing touch.

I know I'm worthy because God will straighten out what I cannot.

GOD REWARDS YOUR SINCERE SEEKING OF HIM

Without faith it is impossible to please and be satisfactory to Him.
For whoever would come near to God must [necessarily]
believe that God exists and that He is the rewarder of
those who earnestly and diligently seek Him [out].
HEBREWS 11:6 AMPC

Hebrews 11 is chock-full of biblical heroes who diligently sought out God, believed and trusted in Him, and followed His ways. Because of their faith, these men and women were rewarded in astounding ways. Yet each was just a regular human being with no special powers and abilities, except those provided by God. They'd seen good times and bad and overcame many obstacles. But their faith never wavered.

Noah followed God's directions and built an ark. Because of his faithfulness, God saved him and his family while the rest of the world was wiped out by a catastrophic flood. Abraham and Sarah, because of their faith, were rewarded with a son in their old age. Motivated by faith, Moses led the Israelites out of Egypt, never wavering in His purpose.

You too have all the qualities and resources you need to be a woman of faith. Seek God, believe and trust in Him, and follow Him, even when you're not sure where He's taking you. As you do, you will be rewarded.

Lord, I firmly believe You exist and reward those who
earnestly seek You. May my faith be pleasing in Your sight!

I know I'm worthy because God rewards my sincere seeking of Him.

GOD'S SPIRIT REDIRECTS YOU

Next Paul and Silas traveled through the area of Phrygia and Galatia, because the Holy Spirit had prevented them from preaching the word in the province of Asia at that time.
ACTS 16:6 NLT

Have you ever had a plan in your head, a course of action you thought it best to follow? Then suddenly you read some scripture, you feel an internal prompting of the Spirit, or you hear a message from a fellow believer, and you're not certain why but you strongly feel you should take a different tack.

That's what happened to Paul and Silas. They'd had a plan, but the Holy Spirit redirected them from Asia, so they went to another area. When they came to the borders of Mysia, they headed north, "but again the Spirit of Jesus did not allow them to go there" (Acts 16:7 NLT). That night, Paul had a vision of a man begging him to go to Macedonia, so they decided to head there right away.

Although you have plans, there will be times when God's Spirit redirects you. For your sake and God's glory, be open to His promptings. He'll never steer you wrong.

I'm determined to be open in heart, mind, body, and soul to Your Spirit's direction. My goal is to allow Your plans to override my own.

I know I'm worthy because God sends His Spirit to redirect me, as needed.

GOD'S WORD GROUNDS
AND BLESSES YOU

*He said to Simon (Peter), Put out into the deep [water], and lower
your nets for a haul. And Simon (Peter) answered, Master, we
toiled all night [exhaustingly] and caught nothing [in our nets].
But on the ground of Your word, I will lower the nets [again].*

LUKE 5:4–5 AMPC

Jesus was preaching and teaching while sitting in one of Simon Peter's boats.
When He stopped talking, He told Peter to take the boat into the deeper
waters and lower his nets. Peter explained how they'd fished all night long
and hadn't caught a thing. Then he said, "But on the ground of Your word, I
will lower the nets [again]."

When Peter did so, he and his fellow fishermen caught so many fish that
their nets were beginning to tear. They asked fellow fishermen in another
boat to help them and filled both the boats with so many fish they were at the
point of sinking. When they reached shore, the fishermen left all to join Jesus.

When you ground yourself on Jesus' Word, following His commands and
promptings, even though they go against logic, you too will find an abundance
of blessings.

*I want You to be Lord of my life, Jesus. May I follow
Your promptings even if I don't really understand them.
For whenever I do, I know I will find a boatload of blessings.*

I know I'm worthy because God's Word grounds and blesses me.

GOD SEES YOUR NEED AND MOVES TO MEET IT

A funeral procession was coming out as he approached the village gate. The young man who had died was a widow's only son, and a large crowd from the village was with her. When the Lord saw her, his heart overflowed with compassion. "Don't cry!" he said.

LUKE 7:12–13 NLT

Jesus and His disciples were walking to the village of Nain. A large crowd followed behind them. It was there He saw a funeral procession. A young man, the bereaved widow's only son and support, had died. When Jesus saw her, His heart gushed with compassion for her. His only words to her were, "Don't cry!" He then went over to the coffin and placed His hands upon it. The men carrying the coffin stood stock-still. Jesus said, "Young man. . .I tell you, get up" (Luke 7:14 NLT). The boy sat up and began talking. "And Jesus gave him back to his mother" (Luke 7:15 NLT).

With one look, Jesus can assess your situation. He sees what you're up against, and His heart goes out to you and overflows with compassion and empathy. He knows what He needs to do, sometimes without your even asking. In this instance, He reunited the heart of a boy and his mother. He knows what you need too. And He's there, watching. Expect Him to move.

You move me, Lord. Thank You for seeing, caring for, and moving in my life.

I know I'm worthy because God sees my every need and moves to meet it.

GOD PROVIDES YOU A SECRET PLACE

He who dwells in the secret place of the Most High shall remain stable and fixed under the shadow of the Almighty [Whose power no foe can withstand]. I will say of the Lord, He is my Refuge and my Fortress, my God; on Him I lean and rely, and in Him I [confidently] trust!
PSALM 91:1-2 AMPC

When you dwell in the secret place that God provides just for you, God will protect you day and night from all dangers (see Psalm 91:3-8). His angels will guard you (see Psalm 91:9-13). And because He loves you, God will deliver you (see Psalm 91:14-16).

But what is this place? It's a place where you reside with the God who is almighty, "Whose power no foe can withstand"—seen or unseen. Where you're safe under His "shadow," a metaphor for His care and protection. Where you affirm aloud, "The Lord is my refuge"—a place of security. "The Lord is my fortress"—protection from attack. "In Him I lean and rely on and totally trust Him."

Dwell in the secret place of God, and find the respite your soul longs for. As you do, He will deliver you, love you, and honor you. You have nothing to lose and everything to gain!

Lord, today I come to You, ready to live in that secret place of peace, protection, and love.

I know I'm worthy because God provides a secret place just for me.

GOD GIVES YOU SECOND CHANCES

"I sank beneath the waves, and the waters closed over me. Seaweed wrapped itself around my head. . . . As my life was slipping away, I remembered the LORD. And my earnest prayer went out to you in your holy Temple."

JONAH 2:5, 7 NLT

God called Jonah to go to Nineveh and announce His judgment upon the wicked city and its people. But instead of going to Nineveh, Jonah headed in the opposite direction to "get away from the LORD" (Jonah 1:3 NLT). He boarded a ship then promptly fell asleep in its hold. God created a huge storm that was only calmed by the sailors throwing Jonah into the sea, and then God caused a huge fish to swallow Jonah.

While down in the fish's belly, Jonah prayed to God for deliverance, so God had the fish vomit him onto the shore. Then God spoke to Jonah a second time, reiterating His initial instructions.

This time Jonah obeyed and announced God's judgment on Nineveh. But when the people turned from their wicked ways, God, in His compassion, relented.

When you disobey God, there's no doubt you'll feel the effects, the consequences of your original waywardness. Yet because of His great compassion, God will give you a second chance. Your mission: take it!

Show me, Lord, where I might have missed an opportunity to serve You. Then, in Your compassion, please give me a second chance!

I know I'm worthy because God gives me second chances.

GOD LIFTS YOU HIGHER

*Hear my cry, O God; give heed to my prayer. From the
end of the earth I call to You when my heart is faint;
lead me to the rock that is higher than I. For You have been
a refuge for me, a tower of strength against the enemy.*
PSALM 61:1–3 NASB

When you're in dire straits, when you are overwhelmed, when you're weak of body and faint of heart and spirit, when you can't seem to get out of your own head, you need God. He's the only one who can give you a new perspective, shield you from the darkness, cover you with His peace, deliver you from your enemies, and give you the breathing room you need. But sometimes you cannot get that "lift" of spirit on your own. You need God's help. So pray. Cry out to God for help. Ask Him to lead you, to lift you to that rock that is so much higher than you—Christ's presence.

As God lifted Moses and put him in a cleft of the rock as His glory passed by (see Exodus 33:22), God will lift you and settle you down on that rock, that "higher place" you cannot reach, keeping you safe until you're once again secure in Him, your strength regained, your heart at peace, and your vision clear.

Lord, I need Your strength, peace, and safety. Lift me to that high rock.

I know I'm worthy because God lifts me higher.

GOD SPEAKS IN YOUR SILENCE

*For God alone my soul waits in silence; from Him comes my
salvation. He only is my Rock and my Salvation, my Defense
and my Fortress. . . . My soul, wait only upon God and silently
submit to Him; for my hope and expectation are from Him.*
PSALM 62:1–2, 5 AMPC

The world is a very noisy place, full of distractions. When you attempt to sit
down with God, the noise of traffic, people's voices, TVs blaring, and barking
dogs can seep through. Once you get yourself to ignore those sounds, the
internal dialogue begins as you start thinking about all the phone calls, emails,
and texts you need to respond to and the to-do list you're determined to
complete. With all that's going on, it's hard to find a moment of peace, much
less silence. But silence—within and without—is what you need to hear God
speak (see Zephaniah 1:7; Habakkuk 2:20). For God isn't in all the noise. He's
"[a sound of gentle stillness and] a still, small voice" (1 Kings 19:12 AMPC).

Even King David had trouble. He begins Psalm 62 by saying his soul is
waiting in silence. But by verse 5 he's *commanding* it to be silent. And that's
just what you may have to do. It is possible. It just takes time, patience, and
practice. Why not start today?

---

*My soul waits in silence before You, God, for You
alone bring hope, peace, and a good word.*

I know I'm worthy because God speaks in my silence.

GOD GIVES YOU SANCTUARY

*But when I considered how to understand this, it was
too great an effort for me and too painful until I went
into the sanctuary of God; then I understood.*
PSALM 73:16–17 AMPC

Sometimes there are some life questions that you just can't figure out. You try to let them go, but they just keep coming back into your mind. It's enough to give you a headache. When this happens, the first and best path for you is to go to God's sanctuary. For the Israelites, that would've been the temple, where God's presence resided. For you, it may be your church or your prayer closet (see Matthew 6:6) where you meet alone with God.

You really don't even have to pose your question. God already knows what's on your mind. The point is to go to God. He'll open the door of understanding to you, give you His wisdom via His Word or His voice as He speaks to your spirit. While you're in His presence, focusing on Him, you can be sure God will guide you with His counsel (see Psalm 73:24). And while you're there, He'll strengthen your heart as well (see Psalm 73:26).

*Lord, I have a question that's been on my mind lately.
And I can't seem to find the answer, so here I am before You.
Help me understand, and then strengthen my heart.*

I know I'm worthy because God gives me sanctuary.

GOD NOURISHES YOU WITH HIDDEN MANNA

I have food (nourishment) to eat of which you know nothing and have no idea. . . . My food (nourishment) is to do the will (pleasure) of Him Who sent Me and to accomplish and completely finish His work.
JOHN 4:32, 34 AMPC

* * * * * * * * * * * * *

Jesus and the disciples had been walking a long way. When they had to pass through Samaria, Jesus, "tired as He was from His journey, sat down [to rest] by the well" (John 4:6 AMPC) while the disciples went to buy food. Even though Jesus, the Word that had become flesh (see John 1:14), was totally exhausted, He had a long conversation with a Samaritan woman and changed her life!

When the disciples came back and urged Jesus to eat the food they'd brought, He said He had food they knew nothing about! They wondered if someone else had brought Him food while they'd been gone. But Jesus explained that His nourishment came from doing God's will!

You also have access to God's hidden manna. So, even when you're weary, don't shrink from doing God's work, the things that please Him. For as soon as you begin, God will not only nourish but revive and refresh your mind, body, spirit, and soul!

I want to please You, Lord. So even when I'm tired, I will seek to do Your will, knowing You will supply all the nourishment I need as I do so.

I know I'm worthy because God nourishes me with hidden manna.

GOD SHOWS YOU THE PATH OF LIFE

*I said to the LORD, "You are my Master! Every good thing I have
comes from you."... You will show me the way of life, granting me
the joy of your presence and the pleasures of living with you forever.*
PSALM 16:2, 11 NLT

God is delighted to show you the way of life in Him. He counsels you in His Word, prompts you through the Holy Spirit, and has given you Jesus as an example so you'll know the way He wants you to go. So, when you come to a fork in the road, God, your eternal guide, will give you all the direction you need to keep you on the right road, leading you to the ramp that leads to His presence and delight while you're on the earth and the one you'll proceed upon after death as you ride on into heaven. "For this God is our God forever and ever; He will be our guide [even] until death" (Psalm 48:14 AMPC).

To that end, always set the Lord before you. Never deviate from His whisper, nudging, and road map to ensure you don't deviate from His way and will for you, and continue on the road in the light of His presence.

---

*Help me, Lord, to be alert to Your signals and
signposts as I ride this eternal way of life with You!*

I know I'm worthy because God shows me the path of life.

GOD WILL NEVER LET YOU BE SHAKEN

I have set the LORD continually before me; because He is at my right hand, I will not be shaken. Therefore my heart is glad and my glory rejoices; my flesh also will dwell securely.

PSALM 16:8–9 NASB

Sometimes you may feel as if you have to reach out for God to find Him, yet He is never far from you (see Acts 17:27). If you are to have Him close, to see Him clearly, even through the mists of life, you must endeavor to have God continually before you. To put out your hand and pull Him close. That means not letting worldly problems, wealth and sorrow, duties and cares, ambitions and responsibilities, push Him out of your mind and heart.

When you make the conscious effort of keeping God continually before you, at your right hand, nothing in life will stress you. No loss or sorrow, no urgency or attack, no person, place, or material thing will shake you. That's what will give you joy in your heart and give you the security you need to live as God would have you live and to calmly and gladly do the tasks He has set before you, the ones that delight Him.

Keep the Lord close, and let all else be. With God, you can have that peace beyond understanding or surpassing.

Lord, I'm putting out my hand and drawing You close. Ah, what peace!

I know I'm worthy because God's presence keeps me steady.

GOD BRINGS YOU TO A PLACE OF ABUNDANCE

We went through fire and through water, but You brought us out into a broad, moist place [to abundance and refreshment and the open air]. . . . He brought me forth also into a large place. . . because He was pleased with me and delighted in me.
PSALM 66:12; 18:19 AMPC

Life is not without its trials, sticky situations, and happenings that appear to be catastrophic at times. Yet while you're in those places, you can be sure God is with you, shielding, comforting, strengthening, and preparing to rescue you. He *will* pluck you out and gently set you down in a broad place, one that's wide enough for your feet to stand secure upon. There you'll find all you need to replenish and restore your heart, mind, body, spirit, and soul.

God is keen to deliver you because He's not only pleased but delighted with you. He loves your face, form, smile, generosity, and quirky sense of humor, your joy of life in Him. So no matter what's going on in your life, breathe easy. God *will* bring you out into the open air.

Sometimes, Lord, I feel as if I'm drowning. Help me remember that no matter where I am, You are with me and will soon pluck me out of trouble and lead me to a place where I can breathe once more!

I know I'm worthy because God plucks me out of trouble and sets me down in a pleasant place.

GOD DAILY BEARS YOUR BURDENS

*Blessed be the Lord, Who bears our burdens and carries
us day by day, even the God Who is our salvation!
Selah [pause, and calmly think of that]!*
PSALM 68:19 AMPC

It's so easy to take things for granted—the food you eat each day, the home that shelters you from the storm, the car that safely takes you to work, the children who run into your arms, the man who smiles at you with love, the dog who wags its tail whenever you come through the door, the work that enables you to buy groceries, the legs that take you from place to place, the water that flows through your spigot, the friends that provide endless support, the siblings that are always there. The list goes on and on!

Yet God not only provides for you, carrying you safely through each day, but He also bears your burdens! Keep this in mind today and every day. Lift up your voice in praise and gratitude to Father God for the care, protection, and bearing of burdens He provides. Blessed be the Lord!

---

*Thank You, Lord, for the way You take care of me every
single day, bearing my troubles, providing everything
I want and need, loving me, carrying me. My heart
overflows with love for You! You are an awesome God!*

I know I'm worthy because God carries
and cares for me every hour of every day!

GOD GUARDS YOUR HEART AND MIND

Don't worry about anything; instead, pray about everything.
Tell God what you need, and thank him for all he has done. Then you will
experience God's peace, which exceeds anything we can understand.
His peace will guard your hearts and minds as you live in Christ Jesus.
PHILIPPIANS 4:6–7 NLT

There are so many things you don't have control over—people, events, organizations, governments, weather, and sometimes even your very self. That's why the apostle Paul tells you to hand everything over to God, the one who *does* have control over absolutely everything. Paul tells you to pray about *all* the things you're concerned about. There is nothing too little for God to pay attention to and nothing too big for Him to handle.

After you tell God all your concerns and things that you need, don't forget to thank Him. It's only then that you'll feel His peace come over you. You'll then enter into your day or close out your night with a heart that is supernaturally calm and a mind that's settled, enabling you to focus on and see what God would have you do and say.

I don't want to leave this place until I've handed all my concerns over to You, Lord. Take these burdens, good God. Please provide these needs. Thank You for all You have done above and beyond my expectations.

I know I'm worthy because God guards my heart and mind.

GOD WANTS YOUR ATTENTION

Eli told Samuel, "Go and lie down, and if he calls you, say, 'Speak, Lord, for your servant is listening.'" So Samuel went and lay down in his place. The Lord came and stood there, calling as at the other times, "Samuel! Samuel!" Then Samuel said, "Speak, for your servant is listening."

1 SAMUEL 3:9–10 NIV

When your need is great, you may be quick to run to God, pour out your troubles, and then wait for Him to speak to you. Yet God doesn't just want your attention when things aren't going well. He wants your ears open to His voice, your heart open to His plans, each and every day.

In those daily quiet moments, when, in that special place, you come before Him in prayer, surrendered to His will and open to His way, say, "Speak, Lord. Your servant is listening." Then actually wait. Listen. Expect God to speak, to tell you that day's message. And in that silence, you will hear His voice. It may be a Bible verse that has touched your heart or the refrain of a hymn or worship song He wants you to take note of. The point is: keep your line of communication open between heaven and earth.

Here I am, Lord. Speak. Your servant is listening. Convey Your message to my open heart and willing spirit as I silently wait before You.

I know I'm worthy because God wants my attention.

GOD'S SPIRIT STRENGTHENS YOUR INNER WOMAN

May He grant you out of the rich treasury of His glory to be strengthened and reinforced with mighty power in the inner man by the [Holy] Spirit [Himself indwelling your innermost being and personality].
EPHESIANS 3:16 AMPC

From God's unlimited resources, He empowers your inner woman with all the strength and reinforcement you need. God does this with the same power He used to resurrect Jesus from the dead! The vehicle through which He does this is His Spirit, the Holy Spirit that came to dwell in you when you first believed in and accepted Jesus through faith.

When you determine to study God's Word, understand it, and live by it, your inner woman—your soul, spirit, mind, and personality—becomes stronger and stronger. You then have the unlimited power to live in hope, faith, and love and to do all that God is calling you to do without fainting or fearing.

This prayer of Paul's for yesterday's believers applies to you today. It reminds you of God's divine power that has its seat in and affects your entire inner life. Be cognizant of this unlimited strengthening and reinforcing power of God, knowing that God continues to supply it through His Spirit to your very core.

All the strength You have given me, Lord, constantly amazes me. Help me be more and more conscious of the unlimited power that dwells so deep within me.

I know I'm worthy because God's Spirit strengthens my inner core with resurrection power!

GOD DOES FOR YOU MORE THAN YOU CAN IMAGINE

Now to Him Who, by (in consequence of) the [action of His] power that is at work within us, is able to [carry out His purpose and] do superabundantly, far over and above all that we [dare] ask or think [infinitely beyond our highest prayers, desires, thoughts, hopes, or dreams]—to Him be glory.
EPHESIANS 3:20–21 AMPC

Christ came into your heart when you accepted Jesus. But He's most at home in those hearts that are dedicated to Him. Those hearts that are "rooted deep in love *and* founded *securely* on love" (Ephesians 3:17 AMPC, emphasis added). The hearts that actually grasp the extent of God's love (see Ephesians 3:18), using the limitless supply of God's love to love others. For then they become flooded with "all the fullness of God" (Ephesians 3:19 AMPC).

When you combine your knowledge of and faith in the Spirit that strengthens your inner woman, are secure in Christ's love, and are flooded within by God Himself, that is when you find that God's unlimited power at work within you enables Him to do more than you ever imagined, hoped, or dreamed! He accomplishes things far beyond your highest prayers to Him! What a limitless strengthening, loving, and powerful God you serve!

I want to realize Your Spirit's strengthening of my inner being, to realize Christ's immense love, and to be filled with You, Lord! Work in me beyond my dreams and hopes!

> I know I'm worthy because God does more within me than I can possibly imagine!

GOD REWARDS YOUR PERSISTENT PRAYERS

Elijah. . .bowed low to the ground and prayed with his face between his knees. Then he said to his servant, "Go and look out toward the sea." The servant went and looked, then returned to Elijah and said, "I didn't see anything." Seven times Elijah told him to go and look.
1 KINGS 18:42–43 NLT

God had just instantly answered Elijah's prayer, sending down fire to burn up water-soaked wood (see 1 Kings 18:37–39). Now Elijah was telling King Ahab, "Go get something to eat and drink, for I hear a mighty rainstorm coming!" (1 Kings 18:41 NLT). Those were faith-filled words, considering it hadn't rained in Israel for three years!

While Ahab ate, Elijah prayed for rain. He sent his servant to go look for it to come—seven times. Finally, the seventh time, the servant came back and told Elijah he saw a little cloud, just the size of a man's fist, rising up out of the sea. And a terrific rainstorm followed.

God will grant your petitions either sooner or later, so don't give up! Remember, the vision will be fulfilled. "If it seems slow in coming, wait patiently, for it will surely take place" (Habakkuk 2:3 NLT).

Lord, help me be a patient and persistent prayer, filled with faith that You will fulfill my expectations. In You I need never give up!

I know I'm worthy because God rewards my persistent prayers.

GOD WILL MEET YOU WHERE YOU ARE

As he was sleeping, an angel touched him and told him,
"Get up and eat!" . . . Then the angel of the LORD came
again and touched him and said, "Get up and eat some
more, or the journey ahead will be too much for you."
1 KINGS 19:5, 7 NLT

Elijah had just put the Baal prophets to shame after God answered his prayer. Then he prayed for rain—and it came. But when Queen Jezebel threatened his life, Elijah, filled with fear, took off. After a day's journey, he was so discouraged that he told God to take his life. Then, exhausted, he fell asleep. But an angel woke him, telling him to eat. Elijah discovered a warm cake of bread and a jar of water. So he ate and drank then fell asleep, only to be awakened and replenished by the angel a second time. "The food gave him enough strength to travel forty days and forty nights to Mount Sinai" (1 Kings 19:8 NLT), where he then heard the still, small voice of God (v. 12).

When, after mountaintop experiences, you're in the valley of despair, God will replenish you until you can continue your journey and once more hear His still, small voice.

Thank You, Lord, for meeting me where I am,
giving me what I need to go on my journey to You.

I know I'm worthy because God replenishes
me so I can continue on in Him.

GOD COMES THROUGH ON HIS PROMISES TO YOU

"God is not a man, so he does not lie. He is not human, so he does not change his mind. Has he ever spoken and failed to act? Has he ever promised and not carried it through?"
NUMBERS 23:19 NLT

You can count on God to always come through on the promises He makes.

God promised Abraham and Sarah they'd have a child in their old age—and Isaac was born (see Genesis 21). He promised Manoah's wife she'd have a son—and Samson was born (see Judges 13). God promised He'd bring His people to a land filled with milk and honey—and He did (see Joshua 5:6). The promises-fulfilled list goes on and on.

Your God, who vows He'll never leave or forsake you (see Deuteronomy 31:6, 8), continues to keep His promises through Jesus who said, "And be sure of this: I am with you always, even to the end of the age" (Matthew 28:20 NLT).

To build up your faith and realize how much you matter to God, make a list of all God's promises. Then claim them one by one, following the advice of Hebrews 10:23 (NLT): "Let us hold tightly without wavering to the hope we affirm, for God can be trusted to keep his promise."

Lord, in a world where no one seems to be true to his word, I know I can count on You to keep Your promises to me. And in them I put all my hope!

I know I'm worthy because God keeps His promises to me.

GOD GIVES BACK WHAT YOU GIVE OUT

Give, and [gifts] will be given to you; good measure, pressed down, shaken together, and running over, will they pour into [the pouch formed by] the bosom [of your robe and used as a bag]. For with the measure you deal out [with the measure you use when you confer benefits on others], it will be measured back to you.

Luke 6:38 AMPC

• • • • • • • • • • • • • • • • •

There is no way in heaven or on earth that you can outgive God. It's absolutely impossible! In the verse above, Jesus says what gifts you give out will be given back to you—and, at times, even more!

When Peter tells Jesus that they'd left their homes to follow Him, Jesus replied, "No one who has sacrificed home, spouse, brothers and sisters, parents, children—whatever—will lose out. It will all come back multiplied many times over in your lifetime. And then the bonus of eternal life!" (Luke 18:29–30 MSG).

It works the same way with what money you offer to God. When you bring all your tithes into the storehouse, God says, "I will open the windows of heaven for you. I will pour out a blessing so great you won't have enough room to take it in! Try it! Put me to the test!" (Malachi 3:10 NLT).

So don't focus on your lack. Instead be generous in your gifts, your dedication, and your tithes. You'll be paid back in full—and more!

You're so generous to me, Lord, spurring me on to give and give, knowing You'll keep me in the black!

I know I'm worthy because God gives me back what I give out!

GOD SHINES HIS PRESENCE UPON YOU

The Lord bless you and watch, guard, and keep you; the Lord make His face to shine upon and enlighten you and be gracious (kind, merciful, and giving favor) to you; the Lord lift up His [approving] countenance upon you and give you peace (tranquility of heart and life continually).
NUMBERS 6:24-26 AMPC

This famous blessing was given by God to Moses. God told him that this was the blessing the priests were to say over His people. And it's the blessing you can claim for yourself today.

God loves to bless you, giving you all you need to live and more, including His very presence. He wants you to know He and His angels are watching over you, guarding and protecting you. God is smiling down upon you; His presence is like a ray of sunshine, giving you love and light for your path. He longs to be kind to you and favor you. He does see you, notice you, and treat you as a favored daughter. And the peace He covers you with is not just serenity in the time of trouble but a feeling of total well-being.

Precious daughter, claim this blessing from your loving God, because you matter to Him.

Lord, You are the sunshine that brightens up my life, lifts my spirit, and makes me whole. Thank You for loving me more than any other. I praise Your name!

I know I'm worthy because God shines His very presence upon me, blessing me and giving me peace.

SCRIPTURE INDEX

OLD TESTAMENT